HORSES
HEARTACHE & HEALING

ELIZABETH DENNISS

Credits
Photos by Fran Jackson, Bob Langrish, Ross Quartermaine, Dianne Robertson, and Katherine Waddington

Chapter 1 photo credit, Ross Quartermaine.

Excerpts by Dr Sheila Greenwell MRCVS; BVM&S

Cover Photograph Courtesy of Katherine Waddington

Proof Reading and Copy Formatting by Lisa Mahoney

Publishing Coaching and Consultation by Do-It-Yourself-Publishing (A Division of Pick-a-WooWoo Publishing Group)

National Library of Australia Cataloguing-in-Publication entry
Title: Horses, heartache and healing : 9 / photos by Fran Jackson, Bob Langrish, Ross Quartermaine, Dianne Robertson, and Katherine Waddington ; excerpts by Dr Sheila Greenwell.

ISBN: 9780992548605 (hardback)
ISBN: 9780992548629 (paperback)
ISBN: 9780992548612 (ebook)

Subjects: Wild horses--Australia.
Waler horse--Australia.
Animal rescue--Australia.
Animal welfare--Australia.
Human-animal relationships--Australia.
Animals--Therapeutic use--Australia.
Horses--Pictorial works.

Other Authors/Contributors:
Jackson, Fran, photographer.
Langrish, Bob, photographer.
Quartermaine, Ross, photographer.
Robertson, Dianne, photographer.
Waddington, Katherine, photographer.
Greenwell, Sheila, writer of supplementary textual content.
Dewey Number: 636.100994
Email: elizabeth@rafalifejourney.com
Web: www.rafalifejourney.com

Dedication

For Sophie, my inspiration

For Monty, my joy

For Mum, my safe place

For Elohim, Creator of All

Acknowledgements

Sophie and I have shared this journey with countless guides and friends (both human and equine) over the past nine years. However I could not have experienced or written this story without Sophie. She continues to inspire and teach me every single day.

I would not have the privilege of knowing Sophie if it were not for Sheila Greenwell, the amazing woman who rescued her from the desert. There are no words to express my gratitude for her tireless efforts to make the world a better place for all horses, including my Sophie (and my Lilly).

I could not have survived the ups and downs of my journey with Sophie without the wisdom, love, support and guidance extended to me by both Kevin and Katherine Waddington. Katherine's beautiful photographs add a depth to this book that cannot be expressed in words and Kevin's exceptional guidance in training Sophie has added a depth to our journey that also cannot be expressed in words.

The support from vets and equine professionals along the way including Sheila Greenwell, Simone Herbert, David Murphy and the equine team at Murdoch University Veterinary Hospital, Bruce Ferguson and Sietske Noble has contributed to the story, to the journey.

The inspiration of Franklin Levinson, Sally Francis, Elaine Hughes and Cathy Prior for opening up the world of equine facilitated learning and empowering me to take the therapeutic benefits of horses to the world is, I hope, an ongoing legacy to their passion and commitment to make the world a better place for humans and horses.

I also acknowledge the dedication of the horsewomen who embraced equine facilitated learning in my own community and who volunteered thousands of hours to help deliver one of the first long term programs in the country – Vicki Mills-Borley, Tina McDonald, Kerry Middlebosch, Rowan Pritchard, Sue Reimers, Megan Richards and Alex Stirling.

Sophie inspired me to start documenting our journey in 2007 and the story has been a work in progress ever since, I was never quite sure where it would end.

The conclusion came with the loss of another beloved animal companion, my canine soul mate Monty. Writing the concluding chapter to this story enabled me to process my grief at losing him and to begin to recover from that loss.

And finally, Mum. You must be acknowledged. I know you do not always understand me but your love and support has provided the springboard to all my life endeavours.

When I look into the eyes of an animal I do not see an animal. I see a living being. I see a friend. I see a soul.

A. D. Williams

Contents Page

Foreword

I think only people who have actually experienced certain things in life are qualified to really discuss those things. Certainly fiction writers can tell a story of pain and suffering or joy and happiness using their imaginations and metaphors from their own experiences. Those stories may be interesting, engaging and even entertaining. But the person who lived the specific experiences and then writes about them tends to provide a more authentic, realistic and personal story. That person may or may not be a great writer and that can make a difference in how the story is told and how it is received by a reader. Interesting or moving life experiences may, or may not, make such a good book depending on the abilities of the author. The combination of a compelling and rather unusual story coupled with good talent as a writer and story-teller can produce a book that is not only a good read, but one that can inform, inspire and uplift those who read it. *Horses, Heartache & Healing* by Elizabeth Denniss I feel is such a book.

So many young girls have fantasized about, wished for and prayed to have a horse of their own. The vast majority never see that wish fulfilled. Those who do manage to realize their dream coming true often have to endure many disappointments, set backs, frustrations and put in long hours of hard work. In other words they had to pay some dues. Elizabeth is no different in this way. But she is very different in certain innate abilities and attributes she possesses. Those attributes include an abundance of compassion, empathy, kindness, intelligence and down right common sense. Another quality I think Elizabeth displays within these pages is a tenacity born out of desire to extend authentic love not just to others, but to herself as well. She tells the story of her struggle with finding her authentic self. Like so many others, including me, emotions, emotional intelligence and emotional congruity were a mystery. Even now, having entered into my senior years, I can occasionally struggle with my willingness for self-love. I can still doubt my worthiness. I do not think Elizabeth and I are alone in this situation. This is another reason I feel this book is so good. It touches upon issues that so many of us have had to, or continue to deal with in our lives.

Horses share many of the same emotions as humans. I have had a few hundred horses in my life and I can attest to that. Sophie, the main equine described in this book, saw her mother mare struggle and die while stuck in a muddy bog. Sophie was just a few months old at the time. Then adding to that, the foal nearly starved to death. We can only imagine the considerable trauma this baby had to face and endure. Then, along comes Elizabeth and so begins a journey with this rescued foal named Sophie. Back then Elizabeth did not have so much experience with horses. She just knew that having her own horse was a dream that she had to materialize in real time and this skinny, pitiful looking little foal was to be it.

Of course getting a horse may have been the easier part of the story. What follows is truly an adventure of the heart, commitment, responsibility and personal strength for both horse and human. Life threatening illness, dangerous surgeries, location issues, relationships, money matters and more unfold within these pages. Another question that arises is after all they have gone through what's next for Elizabeth and Sophie? Finding out the answer to this is an adventure in itself.

I was honoured to be asked to provide a foreword for this book. Honoured because of the admiration and respect I have for Elizabeth Denniss. After reading this book my initial delight as a reader was magnified by the opportunity of being able to share my thoughts about it and its author.

Franklin Levinson

Preface

I always wanted to write a book about horses. As a child I wrote many pony stories complete with self illustrations. As an adult, it seems egotistical to write a story about my own journey. I do not think my life is exceptional. I do however think that it is the stories of every day people, overcoming challenges and adversity that have the capacity to inspire others and make the world a better place – not because the story tellers are heroes, but because we are flawed.

I have never been inspired by perfectionism. I have been inspired by authentic people living their dreams, no matter how simple or mundane those dreams may be considered by 'Hollywood standards'.

My dream was to own a horse of my own. If possible, a wild born horse. I was blessed to live that dream and in doing so I was led into an authentic life. I share the story now to honour my horse, Sophie and to express gratitude for my simple, abundant life. I hope that in sharing our journey we can help, teach and encourage others who are in the midst of their own tumultuous life journey.

I wish you safe passage, and in time, a safe place to dock. May you be blessed with friends and guides to share your journey – and I thank you for reading our story.

Prologue

Sophie's foal was born in the early hours of the morning on 23 August 2013. The wild born mares from Earaheedy Station always give birth in the pre dawn darkness. Katherine's father passed away in the early hours of the same morning, five days after I had lost my beloved two and half year old puppy, Monty. I guess it was no surprise that when I drove up the driveway to the farm, and saw Sophie in the round yard with her newborn colt, that I burst into tears. It had been amazing journey lasting eight years to the month.

As a child I grew up reading Elaine Mitchell's Silver Brumby series. The highlight of my weekends, usually spent with my Dad, would be trips into Perth city on the bus to a tiny book store in London Court. There I would be allowed to purchase the next book in the series. I nagged both my parents until I was finally allowed riding lessons on a regular basis.

"It's just a horse," is a phrase I have grown up with all my life and one I have never understood. I seemed to hear the language of animals clearer, and with less confusion, than that of humans. I didn't understand as a child that this was largely due to the honesty that exists in animal communication that is often lacking in human exchanges, where body language can contradict the spoken word. The happiest hours of my childhood were spent on the back of a horse at a local riding school. For me 'it' was never 'just' a horse. I found most horses far better people than most people. Horses were kind, unhurried and accepting.

The connection with horses ceased in my 20's as I became caught up in work, socializing and pursuing materialistic goals that promised a fulfilment that never came. Then, after travelling the world, having a successful career and a failed marriage, horses came back into my life in a most unusual way.

Chapter 1

WILD HORSE RESCUE

In 2005 two work colleagues, Kevin and Katherine Waddington, had been involved in the rescue of 14 wild horses from a drought stricken station near Wiluna. This was wild, rough country in Western Australia's mid north. The horses were saved from certain death by an equine vet who I was later to become friends with, Dr Sheila Greenwell. Sheila had become aware of the plight of these horses and decided, with a stubbornness that belies her short stature and speaks of her Scottish heritage, to do something about it. With a friend and colleague she headed north, sending emails to friends waiting in Margaret River who were preparing for the arrival of the horses after the rescue.

The journey up was uneventful if not hot and long. We decided not to use the air conditioning in the car so we could get acclimatized to the heat –blimey!! Kept sticking to the seat...and drinking water. I may add I am still doing both in great style.

Popped the swags on the dirt for the first night and lo and behold the lightning and thunder arrived and it rained – we ended up sleeping in the cab of the truck for part of the night. I pretended I was on a long haul flight and someone was bringing dinner around soon, and the movies were just about to start. WH conked out with his head on the steering wheel and has had a crick in his neck ever since.

The good thing is that it is so warm that stuff dries out quickly – with a nice even coating of red dust to boot.

Next day we went round the five remaining waterholes, a small one had dried up and there was a foal carcass in it, such a pity. Most of the holes have dead roos in them. Roos dying in their hordes, even with water available, from heat exhaustion. Hard to imagine in an animal adapted to the climate, but they just can't hack it poor loves. Horses and cattle seem to handle the heat quite well.

As a result of the dead roos, who also get munched by wild dogs at the waterholes, the water is putrid in 2 holes, marginal in 2 and almost ok in one called Ian's Dam where most of the horses are drinking – who can blame them?

So we have been camped here for five days to observe the comings and goings. The bush cover around the dams has been reduced a lot as it has been eaten down. I found a fairly thick, prickly bush which provided good cover about 20m from the dam wall. I have spent literally hours in there... covered in flies which give me the shits no end! The flies are so noisy you can't hear animals approaching. A stallion walked 8m past me and I didn't hear him coming.

I have deduced that roos have lousy sight. They will sit next to you and if they can't hear you or smell you they have no idea! The cattle, of which there are about 50, see and smell well, make a note of you, then carry on with what they were doing anyway. Thank gawd as there are some big bulls there and if they took exception you are done for, nowhere to run and no big trees to shoot up.

The horses see, smell and hear well, the most perceptive of the lot, their level of panic seems to vary greatly between individuals. The chunky stallion in the photos is hyper acute and tries to take his family off but they just dawdle, which drives him nuts.

I have seen four family groups comprising of stallion and 2-3 mares and the youngsters. There is a group of 4 bachelor colts who are very flighty. Then the loners who are the cast offs, one poor old mare who lives alone with a young foal at foot. She came 10m from me and didn't worry, even fell asleep facing away from me. I suspect her days are nearly over and she was kicked out, or couldn't keep up, but happened to be pregnant at the time. Poor old sod, she is about 16hh and her foal will make a lot of height but has an umbilical hernia.

Then there is an old stallion just thin and beaten up. Have seen pictures of him but haven't come across him yet. Last but not least is a lone old stallion with the biggest tumour on the end of his willy. The whole affair hangs below his hocks and he has trouble walking, poor old soul. I saw him only once, we hope to dispatch him as it will be a slow end otherwise.

Our plan of trapping at the dams isn't going to work, there are other holes they can drink from if they are desperate. We put pickets all around Ian's Dam which put most of them off so they went elsewhere, no wire I may add. The cattle just walked through them. The baits didn't work, no one was interested in salt, molasses or even Lucerne hay, eventually the cattle twigged on to the hay so it wouldn't stay there long.

There is no way we can fence off 4 dams and trap at one as we would be cutting off a life support system for so many animals. I still can't believe they are going to perish when it dries up. Unless there is enough rain to fill the clay pans – if there is then we will have to abort the mission as the place turns to sticky mud and you can't get a vehicle in. So the plan is to explore the option of a plane and ground muster.

The horses are in a restricted area due to water availability which helps, but the logistics are a horror due to the terrain. So we are back in civilization (sort of) to see about some organizing.

I wouldn't call this a luxury holiday tour, the temp has averaged 43°C most days with a 46°C the other day, the flies are thick and noisy and the wind blows fire red dust into everything and everywhere. I wake up most mornings with a mouthful of grit, hair like a brillo pad and a water ration of 1 cup to sort it out! I have come to realize that water is the most precious thing on the planet – bugger the gold and diamonds. So if we can muster the labour, hessian, and plane for an aerial effort then that is the plan. Not so ideal for the horses but the topography and small group numbers have beaten us.

So what have I learnt about wild horses? The stallion always leads, the rest of the family usually follow in the same order, his #1 mare is second, then the kids, then another mare at the back if he has one. He drinks first then stands guard when the others are drinking, then he leads them away.

They never drink at the same time as cattle, one or the other hangs back and waits until they are finished, very polite stuff.

Roos take ages to drink and only come in at morning and night, horses come in at any old time, including the middle of the night and not at the same time each day either. Cattle stand in the water, horses hate getting their feet wet! Front feet toes and no more if it can be avoided.

I haven't mentioned colour of horses yet, there are four stallions with families, three are white and the other is such a dark grey that he *looks black, but he has a striking white face. He is a young fellow and has some height about him.*

If we get them all I would bring him and the chunky bloke in the photo back, the other stations around here are horse friendly so I might persuade them to take the other boys to introduce genetic diversity in their small mobs.

No one uses their resident horse mobs, but all are reluctant to get rid of them as there is sentimental attachment to the past, which is great for the horses.

With a considerable amount of support from neighbouring Granite Peaks Station, Sheila managed to pull off an aerial muster with success. Despite the seemingly insurmountable challenges, 14 horses were rescued off the station and brought to Margaret River.

I met these horses weeks after their rescue. It was an awe-inspiring moment to be in the presence of truly wild animals.

What I remember the most about the day I met the Earaheedy horses was their eyes. Despite the hardships in drought, in capture and relocation, in adapting to domestic life, their eyes were filled with gentleness and wisdom. I was spell bound and yearned to be able to provide a home for one of these magnificent animals.

Sheila advised me that all the horses had found homes but that she hoped to undertake a return visit to see if additional horses could be rescued. If she did find more horses, she promised she would try and match me to one of them. A few months later Sheila headed off, again keeping us in the loop via emails.

From Perth I was on the next plane north with my outback survival gear in tow...i.e. a couple of bottles of wine, sun cream, clothes that don't matter and the video primed for action. Sadly, the latter wasn't required, after 3 days of criss-crossing Earaheedy (all million acres of it), it became apparent that there were no horses there. The only remaining water on the west side was restricted to two dams known as Spider's and John's. Both were in a disgusting state as they were full of rotting carcasses which took your breath away if you stayed down wind for too long.

WH and I decided not to waste our trip and to help Jim on Granite Peak with his cattle mustering. Without the help of the locals on the previous trip we wouldn't have caught any horses – we had borrowed panels, trucks, water tanks, raided their beer fridges and stayed socially acceptable by using their showers and domestic facilities. The least we could do was help them with their work. Ross Quartermain was with us again, without his intimate knowledge of the Earaheedy we would probably be stuck out the back somewhere! So we had a week of robust cattle mustering which is not for the faint hearted believe me... those guys know what they are doing...which is just as well as some of those big mickey bulls were intent on having us on the end of their horns! I, for one, was mighty relieved when the road train departed with its load of disgruntled bovines.

By this time WH had to depart for the east again due to work commitments. Ross and I decided to head home the long way – via Earaheedy and the other stations to the south – just in case we saw something. And we did! Four healthy horses near Spider Dam and that made us determined to have another go!

Pressing matters at home called Sheila to the south soon after she had seen the four horses, but she was determined to head back to Earaheedy to try another rescue. Sheila was home for a couple of weeks before heading north for the next rescue attempt.

Those of us who remained behind did not hold out much hope. The situation was dire and the likelihood of any horses surviving the extreme conditions during the intervening weeks seemed impossible. Out of the blue I received an unexpected telephone call, Sheila had found two fillies between 3 and 4 months old under a tree on the station!

The tree was tiny and afforded a minimal amount of protection. The two fillies appeared to have huddled in the shade. Together, in the blistering heat with no food or water they were surrounded by the bleached bones of horses that had sought respite there before them.

On our first day we caught the two orphan foals which we found resting under a tree... to cut a long story short they were so weak we walked up to them pushed them to the trough for a drink – not the handling techniques we were expecting to be using at this stage! To make matters worse we decided it was too dangerous to leave them in the yard for the night as the dingo numbers are running high and they would be easy pickings.

We made a crate on the back of Ross's ute with some spare panels and bodily lifted them up there...easier said than done and it would have been worthy of a photo if we hadn't had all hands up the posterior of the poor foals catapulting them into the ute. They travelled as if they had been doing it all their short lives and were soon back at the safety of Granite Peaks where we rigged up a special kiddies pen with a shade cloth area, water trough and round bale of hay.

Now named Lily and Sophie after Ross's grandmothers, these two took to the good life readily. Poor Lily was the weaker of the two and was on the receiving end of liberal doses of cooking oil and calf milk powder until she got up the steam to tackle the hay. I must add that the jaws on both have never stopped since, and they are going from strength to strength rapidly.

Sheila was able to walk right up to the fillies. They were too weak to care even when every nerve, every instinct, would have been screaming at them to 'run'. She circled the fillies, squatting down to assess them and when she walked back across the ridge towards Ross and the ute Lilly called out and using whatever remaining strength she had, tottered in the same direction before collapsing into an exhausted, dehydrated and starving heap.

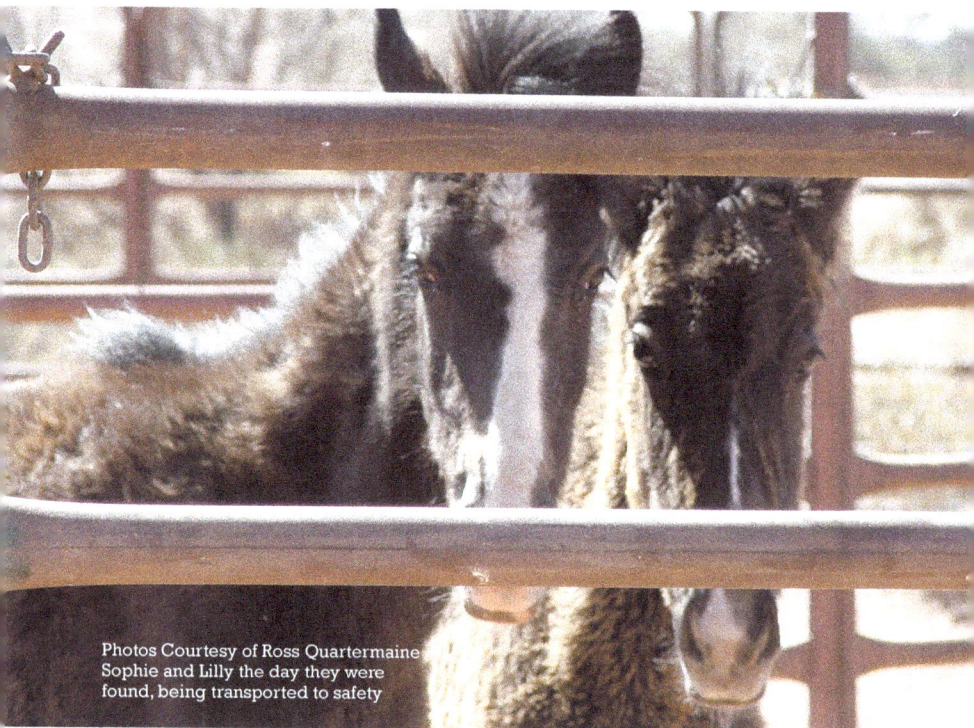

Photos Courtesy of Ross Quartermaine
Sophie and Lilly the day they were
found, being transported to safety

20

Sheila figured that Sophie's mother was a carcass in Spider Dam, that mare and foal had become stuck in the boggy mess at the bottom of the dam, not far from the tree where the two fillies had been found. The wild mare had probably taken her young filly down for a drink from the remaining putrid water, became entrapped in the bog and unable to free herself, had died.

Sophie, whose legs were caked in dry mud when found, probably had continued to suckle until the milk dried up before attempting the extremely steep ascent back up out of the dam. A tremendous effort for a young horse, no doubt traumatized to some degree by watching her mother struggle in the mud and then die.

It remains a mystery where and when Lilly had met up with Sophie. As the two horses have matured, it is clear that they are related and probably from the same mob, sharing the same stallion father. Sheila did not find another mare's body in the vicinity that would account for Lilly's orphaned state.

I have often wondered if the solitary mare with a young foal at foot, observed by Sheila on her first trip to Earaheedy Station was in fact Lilly's mother who had perhaps died prior to Sophie's mother. Both fillies had umbilical hernias when rescued and the time frame would be about right.

Sheila's return to Margaret River after her third rescue mission caused great excitement amongst our circle. In addition to Sophie and Lilly she had also rescued an older colt named Roscoe, a grey mare and black-brown mare.

The grey mare had been named Sweaty Betty by Sheila, and the darker mare was named Darrah by a friend. Sweaty Betty's name was soon changed to Betsy and a general decree passed that Sheila ought not be allowed to name any rescued horses!

Shortly after her return, Sheila and I discussed the future of the

Photo Courtesy of Fran Jackson
Sophie and Lilly in Margaret River

two young orphaned fillies. She offered Sophie to me, explaining that it would be at least 3 months before Sophie recovered enough to leave Sheila's care. I accepted the opportunity to purchase Sophie, knowing that the price asked would scarcely cover her rescue let alone the ongoing veterinary care Sheila was providing.

The day I met Sophie I was filled with both nervous apprehension and excitement and when I first set eyes on her tiny frame I wanted to cry. The largest part of her was her huge brown eyes that appeared to me

Photo Courtesy of
Katherine Waddington
Elizabeth and Sophie first meet

22

to be haunted. Her brown coat was matted, she looked incredibly fragile as she stood behind Lilly.

Sophie and Lilly were kept together at Cape Mentelle Winery in Margaret River. They were being cared for by a lovely lady who leased some acreage from the winery, close to where Sheila lived. I was so overwhelmed by Sophie that it took me several weeks to revisit her. I felt completely unprepared to care for her.

Thankfully Fran was doing a brilliant job, including using a pair of clippers to cut back both fillies coats. The hair was so densely matted that the possibility of grooming out all the knots was impossible.

We were all amazed that these two dinky di born and bred wild fillies stood stock still with the unusual noise and sensation of electric clippers trimming off their 'dreadlocks'. Even before the big trim, Sophie relished a decent brush, grinding her teeth in pleasure when the pressure of the brush promoted circulation. Slowly the two fillies gained weight and in time Sheila removed the hernias they both carried. It was a blessing to be able to leave Sophie with Lilly at the Winery as I had started working at the Shire of Nannup, having left my job at the Shire of Augusta-Margaret River.

I was still living in Margaret River and commuting a 150km round trip, across 72km of gravel track in my little Hyundai every day. The days were long and did not leave me much time for horse pursuits but I knew Sophie was receiving plenty of tender loving care.

Around the same time Katherine and Kevin had decided to sell their 5 acres in Margaret River and purchase a larger property further inland or south. They had purchased several of the Earaheedy horses who were in the process of being assessed for registration by the Waler Horse Society of Australia Inc. Their plan was to develop a small breeding program and a larger property was required to fulfil this dream.

In the meantime I was growing tired of the long commute to work and had become discouraged in looking for a small acreage close to Nannup where Sophie and I could live together. Rental properties of any sort were scarcer than hen's teeth and I began to worry that I might not have a home for Sophie when she was given the all clear from Sheila.

When a colleague left the Shire of Nannup, I was offered the opportunity to rent the house previously tenanted by him. I accepted the offer, even though it was a house in town with no room for a horse.

Once settled in Nannup, the drive back to Margaret River no longer seemed as onerous because I wasn't doing it every day. I had more time and energy to visit Sophie, but I still wanted her closer to me.

The months were passing and I knew I needed to start looking for a place to agist Sophie, but I was reluctant. She and Lilly had shared and survived so much together, it was going to be difficult to separate them.

A former neighbour and friend from Margaret River, Michelle Manners, had decided to buy Lilly so I knew she would be well cared for. I did not have the financial ability to take on the responsibility of both horses as I rebuilt my life in Nannup. I was glad that Lilly would be loved and cared for when the time came for the two young horses to part ways.

Late one afternoon, when I was mulling over the problem of finding a home for Sophie Katherine called me to let me know she and Kevin had put in an offer on a farm located 15 kilometres east of Nannup. She asked if I would like to agist Sophie with them once the settlement and move had taken place. It could not have worked out more perfectly.

I drove out to the property soon after settlement. We were still waiting for Sheila to give Sophie the all clear to move on but I was keen to see Katherine and Kevin's new home. Nestled in a small valley, the 94 acre property delighted me with its beauty and serene, peaceful atmosphere.

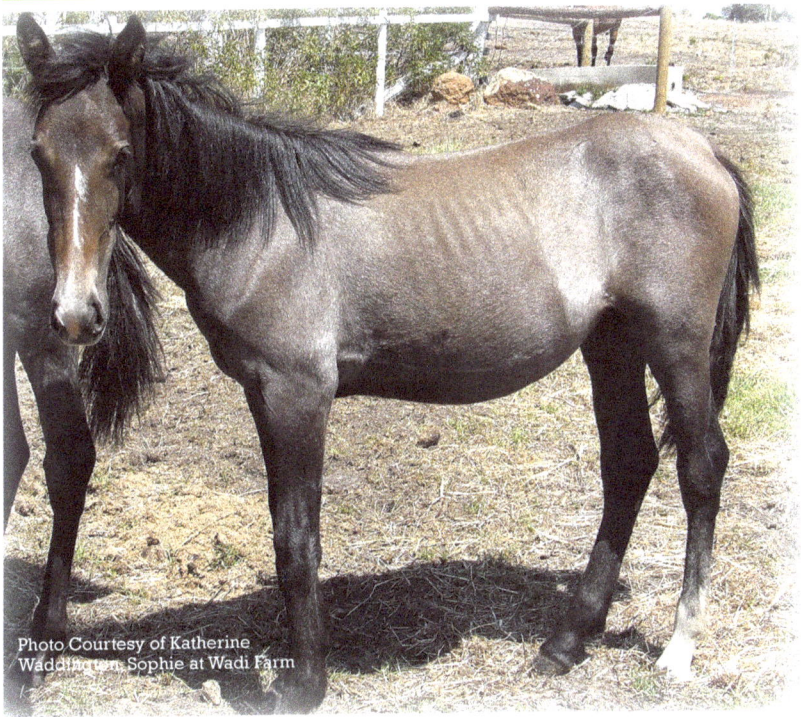

Photo Courtesy of Katherine Waddington, Sophie at Wadi Farm

Photo Courtesy of Katherine Waddington Sophie (right) and Lilly (left) at Wadi Farm

The majestic old growth Karri trees on the property were inspiring and the abundance of native bushland balanced the cleared pasture. The farm house was small and comfortable while the large dam provided essential water to the house and paddocks and added to the peacefulness. I was content knowing that I had found the right home for Sophie.

Three months passed during which time Katherine, Kevin and their horses settled into the new property. Then, in February 2006, Sophie and Lilly arrived at Wadi Farm. Lilly had been Sophie's travelling companion, and stayed a couple of days to ease the separation before returning home to Margaret River.

Within a year of moving and settling at Wadi Farm, Katherine's parents also moved to Nannup. It was both an exciting, and a difficult time for them as her father was diagnosed with dementia and Alzheimer's disease. The ebb and flow of life continued.

Sophie was now 9 months old (or thereabouts) and quite the cutie. The people involved in the original Earaheedy rescue had formed a charity, the Outback Heritage Horse Association of WA Inc, to continue to fundraise and rescue unique 'heritage brumbies'. Being the

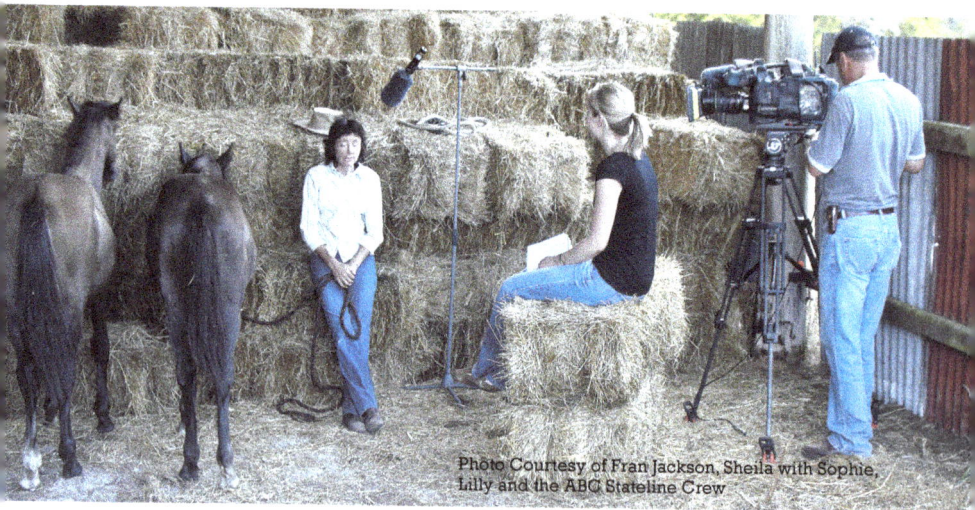

Photo Courtesy of Fran Jackson, Sheila with Sophie, Lilly and the ABC Stateline Crew

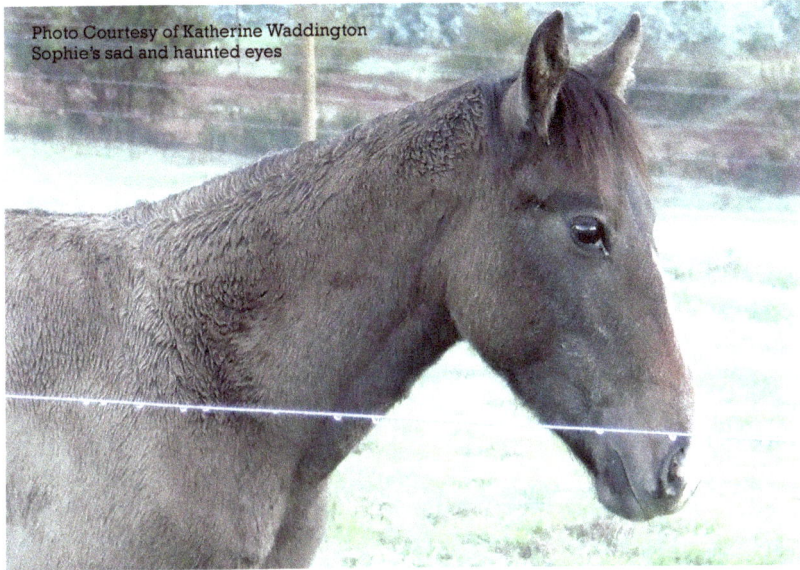

Photo Courtesy of Katherine Waddington
Sophie's sad and haunted eyes

youngest rescued horses Sophie and Lilly attracted a lot of attention.

ABC Stateline featured a story on Sheila's amazing rescue journey to Earaheedy Station and Sophie and Lilly co-starred alongside Sheila in the television footage recorded for the segment.

Katherine and Kevin often had visitors interested in joining the charity or viewing wild bred horses. Sophie was often visited in the paddocks and the usual comment was, "what a darling, but how sad she seems." Her head always hung low and she often had a haunted look in her eye.

I knew there was truth in these observations and began to realize I needed to explore modalities that would help Sophie recover on an emotional level in the same manner we had nourished and restored her on the physical level.

Unbeknown to me we were about to embark on a journey that would teach me just how much there is to a horse, a journey that would help heal my own broken heart.

Chapter 2

THE BEGINNING OF HEALING

When my marriage ended many of my friends told me how brave they thought I was. I remember thinking it was an odd thing to say. I didn't see much bravery in failing in marriage. I found the experience of marriage equal to standing in a circular room with mirrors on every curve of the wall. Everything about me – the good, the bad and the ugly – was clearly reflected back at me in how I reacted to what was, and what wasn't, working in the marriage.

It seemed like I could stay in the relationship only by choosing to block out all of the harmful self truths. This could only be achieved by placing all the blame for the marriage failings on my husband. I tried this for a while, not consciously realizing what I was doing.

Those mirrors however would not go away and after a short period of misery on his part, and mine, I realized I didn't really have a choice but to face up to those truths.

I decided to confront my own fears and limitations and stop blaming my husband for what wasn't working in my own life. I realized I needed to take responsibility for my own happiness and needs, instead of expecting him to fill them. I also began to realize that my husband needed to take responsibility for his own happiness.

It was no longer easier for me to blame others and look outside of myself for my happiness. I found myself unsure as to who I was and what I wanted in life, so I made the commitment to find out. Perhaps this was the act of bravery others could see, but was hidden from me, at the time. I only knew I couldn't continue going through life the same way any more.

For a time I tried to progress my personal growth within the marriage. It soon became apparent that this wasn't going to work. A friend pointed out to me that I had become "both the poison and the cure" for my husband, who now seemed to blame the ongoing tenuous state of our marriage entirely on me.

We committed to seeking counselling, both individually and as a couple. For a while I thought this was helping and it lifted my hopes that we could grow together in our individual journeys and enhance the relationship as a result of both being committed to self development.

I can't say for certain when I realized this was not going to happen. Anger and resentment continued to grow until one day I faced the reality that the quality of my life on every level – emotionally, spiritually, physically, and mentally – was going to be considerably higher without my husband in my life. I made the decision to leave.

I had by this time begun to realize that co-dependency was a contributing factor to the failed marriage. I had, for much of my life, been caretaking others in the hopes that some day, somebody would take care of me. I began to realize that this was not how it worked and was, in fact, quite an unhealthy state of being.

I was quite scared to acknowledge that even if it meant being on my own, for the rest of my life, I needed to take this step and accept being on my own so I could build a healthy relationship with myself. I realized that I could not expect to have a strong and healthy relationship with someone else if I did not have a strong and healthy relationship with my own self.

So I packed and left our home with my books, my music and my clothes and moved into a friend's small, two bedroom cedar home on 6 acres in Margaret River. It was a beautiful, peaceful, rural environment and I spent long hours sitting on the veranda watching the garden, the birds, and the forest or driving the short distance to the beach. I took to taking long, solitary walks on the beach and asking myself what I liked, what I didn't, and in time, what I wanted.

I remembered that I loved horses, and dogs, and neither had been a part of my life for over ten years.

I sadly realized this was because I had not honoured my authentic self. Even as a very small child, all I dreamed of was living in the country, with horses, dogs, chickens and a vegetable garden. Instead I had lived and worked in professional environments in Perth, Melbourne and Sydney. With Sophie in my life, I felt like I was remembering who I was.

Once I had moved and settled into the new house in Nannup, there were mornings I would wake up and remember I had a horse of my very own and I was filled with excitement. There were other mornings I woke up completely overwhelmed by the responsibility.

I was worried that Sophie would have trouble adjusting to her new home and the stress of Lilly leaving. I visited her often and we would spend long hours together. She enjoyed being groomed and I found the experience of brushing her relaxing and calming. I didn't understand at the time how much bonding occurred during those hours of brushing. As my knowledge of horse social and herd behaviour grew, I came to appreciate how important mutual grooming was to the emotional and physical well being of the horse.

During those times I had plenty of time to reflect on my life journey and the amazing blessing of now having Sophie in my life. I would talk as I groomed her, and shared with her the heartbreak of recent years.

The months passed and Sophie continued to develop well physically, despite having been compromised at an early age. Because she was orphaned, and as a result weaned, at a very young age, her body did not receive sufficient vitamins, minerals and other nutrients from her dam's milk that would have supported normal growth and development. She should have matured at approximately 16hh but her hard start to life – the lack of adequate food, water and minerals – had left her stunted with slightly turned in front knees.

Sophie's emotional development was more of an ongoing concern. I had begun to observe the sentient capacity of horses and to realize that grief and loss could be affecting Sophie's emotional development, but I did not know what to do about it.

When Sophie arrived at Wadi Farm she took to shadowing a young two-year-old mare named Norma. This beautiful horse was a yearling herself when rescued with her dam from Earaheedy Station during Sheila's first rescue mission. Norma and Sophie were the two youngest horses on the property and formed a bond that reflected nuances of Sophie's relationship with Lilly.

Sophie was also reunited with Darrah the Dark One, a sweet natured mare who was the only non grey horse rescued from Earaheedy Station. Darrah had been rescued at the same time

as Sophie. The older Earaheedy mares Margaret, Lorna and Ruth continued to provide a connection to their shared past and a healthy herd hierarchy and social environment. Lilly was continuing to be well cared for in Margaret River by the lovely Michelle, who owned the property next door to my friend where I had formerly lived.

I was acutely conscious of how much I did not know about horses. I had asked Kevin, an experienced and gifted horse trainer, to work with me in training Sophie. We commenced Sophie's basic groundwork training during 2006 and while she was quick to learn, she was often only 'there' because she had to be, not entirely because she wanted to be. Sophie often stood off to the side in the paddock, her head bowed low and whenever there was activity on the farm that attracted the attention of other horses she would turn her back in disinterest. The word I often used to describe Sophie was 'detached'.

Photo Courtesy of
Katherine Waddington
Sophie and Elizabeth

One day I decided to have a paddock visit with Sophie, instead of a training session. I spent an hour slowly brushing her from top to tail. I have never seen a horse enjoy her grooming as much as Sophie. This day, the entire time I talked to her about her mother and how horrible it must have been to watch her die in the dam, and how brave Sophie was to climb out all by herself and to find and take care of Lilly. I finished brushing her and stood beside her, my arm around her neck, still speaking of how much I loved her and that I would never leave her, she was part of my family and my life now. As I talked her head dropped lower and lower until it was resting heavily on my shoulder. A couple of hundred kilograms of horse, even when the horse is not fully grown, is a heavy weight to bear but I did not want to break the magic of that moment. I don't know how much of what I told Sophie that day was understood, but a depth of connection was added to our relationship from that time.

Chapter 3

HORSES AS SENTIENT BEINGS

During 2008 Norma was sold, and went to a new home near Perth. Sophie seemed to cope with her departure relatively well, spending more time with Ruth, however she retained a general air of sadness and detachment.

There had been improvements in her state of being over the past 12 months, assisted greatly by the work of an Equine Touch practitioner who had offered to donate her time to provide body work on rescued horses. After observing her work on several horses, and reading up on this modality, I completed my level 1 training and continued to perform regular Equine Touch body work on Sophie. This modality had certainly shifted energies and emotions for her, but there still seemed to be a long way to go.

The Equine Touch involves gentle, hands on moves using finger and thumb, which are performed in a specific sequence. These energy releasing moves stretch and softly manipulate the tissues to assist the horse to relax, release tension and naturally rebalance. The modality also helps with detoxification and lymphatic drainage. What I found especially interesting, in observing Sophie during Equine Touch sessions, was her physical response to the moves. She would lick, chew and sigh, her body and eye softening with the physical and energetic release provided. This was referred to as 'processing'. During her first session she yawned often and extensively, stretching and testing her muscles. The moves gently manipulated tissue and fascia in a non-invasive manner, releasing pain so that her body could create balance. I was sceptical of the capacity of Equine Touch to stimulate energy flow to enable the body's own resources to heal itself. However I could see on the physical level that Sophie was more relaxed and moved with greater freedom as her sessions continued.

Earlier in 2008, the Equine Touch practitioner had posted a photo of Sophie on an equine healer's website and asked for input from colleagues and shamans with different healing modality expertise.

No information regarding her history was provided with the photo. We were amazed by the consistency of responses and suggestions that came from people around the world stating they believed Sophie had suffered a huge physical and emotional trauma at a young age and that it involved death, possibly of her mother.

It was also suggested that she might have issues bonding with either equines or humans as a result of her experiences. I felt very vulnerable to the sudden expanse of possibilities that opened up in relation to energy healing and the depth of equine sentience. As a child I had always imagined that animals could communicate amongst themselves and quite often talked to my animals. As an adult I had never considered the possibility that humans could engage in meaningful communication with another species. Yet it appeared that many healers, who had never met Sophie, could remotely communicate with her to develop awareness of her physical and emotional needs. The awareness that animals were in fact capable of such communication and sentience (appropriate to their species) was overwhelming. I couldn't fully absorb the implications. I could however accept that the experience of learning Equine Touch had opened my mind to accept that energetic and emotional balance was linked to physical health and well-being.

While this helped with theoretic understanding I was dogged by uncertainty as to how to use this information to help Sophie. I wasn't ready to fully explore equine sentience and energetic healing modalities, even though Equine Touch was opening a door. These concepts challenged me because they did not fit comfortably with my adult beliefs and values. I was unable to verbalise to others what I was going through because I struggled to find words to put constructs around ethereal experiences. I was also conscious that in certain social circles such ponderings would be considered unusual at best and ridiculous at worst. As my journey with Sophie continued, it was the renewal of her relationships with Norma and Lilly that enabled me to fully accept the ability of other species to emote, connect and communicate.

Toward the end of 2008, Norma returned unexpectedly to Wadi Farm as her owners had decided she was not the horse for them. Katherine and Kevin always preferred to have horses they had previously owned and sold return if there were problems so they could rehome the horse.

Norma's return lifted Sophie's energy and interest in life and I began to wonder if she had equated Norma's earlier departure with her death. I enjoyed seeing Sophie and Norma reunited and spending time together. All too soon it seemed that Norma had truly found her 'forever home' with Robyn Harrod, a beautiful, big hearted woman from Merredin who had a strong connection with the mare from their first meeting. I was concerned as to how Sophie would react to Norma's second departure from her life.

I discussed my concerns about Sophie with Katherine. I was curious to know her views on the capacity of horses to grieve and bond with each other. I was taken aback when, during that discussion, she asked me, "Has Sophie seen Lilly since they came here together in 2006?"

We looked at each other in amazement as we realized the two survivors had not seen each other in 2 years and that in Sophie's mind, Lilly could well be dead. Perhaps if they were reunited it would help Sophie to further heal. I was on the phone to Michelle that very night asking if Lilly could come for an extended visit, explaining the reason why. Michelle was more than happy to assist and arrangements were made to transport Lilly from Margaret River to Nannup.

Photo Courtesy of Katherine Waddington, Lilly (left) and Sophie (right) reunited

Photo Courtesy of Katherine Waddington, Lilly (rear) and Sophie (fore) with Carranya (right)

While the two horses had both been orphaned at a young age, Lilly had adapted to her new life without displaying emotional trauma. Lilly was a free spirited, happy and contented horse. I eagerly anticipated Lilly's arrival and it was a joy to see what can only be described as complete shock and then utter happiness when Sophie and Lilly laid eyes on and muzzle kissed and sniffed each other.

The two horses were left to roam the big paddock with the rest of the Earaheedy mob. Lilly had some herd etiquette learning to experience and Sophie had the opportunity of learning the sheer joy of living as she and Lilly raced each other across the dam wall just because they could. I watched them together, noting the difference between them and realized Sophie had never had the opportunity to be a young horse. Life had been hard and had been about survival from the beginning for Sophie, with the added responsibility of protecting Lilly as is the way with the more dominant horse.

I could not help but draw some degree of parallel to my own early years and my outlook on life which was also quite serious. My early childhood years were affected by the divorce of my parents and a strong sense, from an early age, of the need to emotionally support others.

After a delightful two week visit Lilly returned to Margaret River. I was sad to see her leave Wadi Farm and to separate her once again from Sophie. Lilly demonstrated an unusually resistant attitude to entering the horse float for the journey home and I wondered if she was reluctant to depart. I was also worried that Sophie might revert to her former solitary ways. I softly whispered to Carranya, Kevin's Kimberley bred gelding, and asked him to take care of her for me. He dutifully and immediately, followed her into the paddock they were currently sharing.

Norma was thriving in her new home, and Robyn committed to bringing her down for spells from time to time so that she could retain the connection with her Earaheedy herd.

The more Sophie's behaviour challenged my notion of the sentient capacity of horses, the more I was forced to face another harsh reality.

I could no longer avoid facing a truth that had begun to reveal itself to me back in the glass encased room that was my marriage. I had completely lost the ability to identify my own emotions and worse, I was in fact afraid of my emotions.

I was beginning to understand the need for emotional awareness as a foundation for an authentic life and as a cornerstone for a connection with another being – including, or perhaps especially, with a horse. I didn't understand why or how but spending more time with horses was helping me reconnect with my own emotional state of being.

I started reading a wide range of works that touched on the growing body of evidence that horses are in fact sentient beings.

That is to say, horses have the capacity to perceive and to feel emotions as well as physical sensations. This view is not shared by all equestrians, however the work of individuals such as Franklin Levinson, Margrit Coates and Linda Kohanov provide compelling arguments to support this view. The development and success of equine facilitated therapy, guided education, leadership and personal development programs further support this view.

Despite my childhood experiences, where I had an easy capacity to engage with animals as beings with feelings of their own, as an adult I found this concept challenging. Yet I had the embodiment of a young, grief stricken horse, in plain sight to challenge any limiting beliefs I held that may have restricted my capacity to be open to this possibility. Sophie had expressed joy in seeing Lilly again. They had recognized each other.

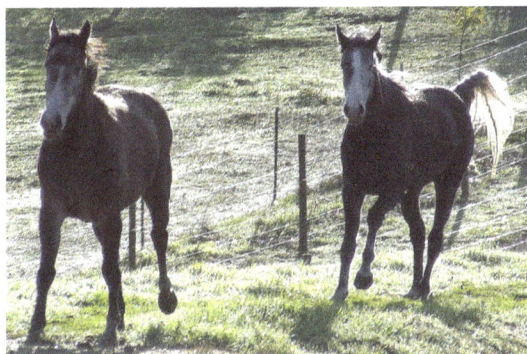

Photo Courtesy of Katherine Waddington, Sophie (fore) and Lilly (rear) at play

Photo Courtesy of Katherine Waddington, Lilly (left) and Sophie (right) at rest

Chapter 4

SAYING GOODBYE

Sophie was the only foal on the property when she arrived in Nannup. Being an orphaned baby in the mob she had a tough time learning her manners and place in the world. It was the older Earaheedy mare, Ruth, who had the most patience with her and it was from Ruth that Sophie learned how the world worked, her place in it, and herd etiquette. Thus began an adjustment phase where Sophie began to integrate into the world, even though she remained distant and closed off in many ways.

When Ruth arrived in Margaret River following the first Earaheedy Station rescue, Sheila estimated Ruth's age at approximately 12 years. Even at 12 she was considered 'old' for a wild horse. Life is not always kind to horses in the wild, the rough conditions and the physical toll of producing a foal each year do not generally allow for a long life.

It took a year of patient work before Ruth developed a level of trust in humans that allowed 'touching'. One day I received a phone call from Katherine, advising me that Sheila had recently assessed Ruth's teeth and the old girl was in fact 24 years of age! We were amazed that a horse of her grace, exceptional movement and strength had been tough enough to survive so long in the wild. Earaheedy Station is a barren, drought stricken place and Ruth had survived it for over two decades. While never fully domesticated, Ruth had adapted to allow humans into her world. She was a grateful recipient of both grooming and body work sessions. She enjoyed human interaction when it suited her and she was never extensively trained or ridden. Ruth's primary role was simply to just be a part of the Earaheedy herd.

Ruth's health seriously deteriorated in the autumn of 2009 and it was the lead mare Margaret who stayed with Ruth as she slowly distanced herself from the rest of the mob.

We knew that time was running out for Ruth and I was concerned by the thought of losing her and the impact her leaving would have on Sophie who, I had come to believe, had experienced strong trauma associated with seeing her own mother die.

Sophie's general demeanour continued to be one of sadness and nothing I did seemed to help her totally move forward. She truly seemed stuck, somewhere. The imminent loss of Ruth and the emotional effect it might have on her worried us all. Finally, not wanting Ruth to have to suffer through the winter, Katherine, Kevin and Sheila decided the time had come to euthanize Ruth who had faced a long battle with heart and lung issues. The night before we were to say goodbye to Ruth, Katherine and Kevin brought her in from the big paddock to the paddock where she was to be buried.

Photo Courtesy of
Katherine Waddington
Earaheedy Ruth

Sophie, Margaret, Lorna and Moonlight (Lorna's filly) were all brought in to spend the night with Ruth. Experience is a great teacher and had taught us that horses do grieve and need time to deal with death.

When I arrived at the farm that morning, Sheila was not yet there. Katherine, Kevin and I chatted while we waited in the warm autumn sunshine. The energy at the farm was different today. The horses could tell something was happening and by the time Sheila arrived and we headed down to the northern end of the paddock where Ruth and the mob were, our movements were monitored by equine eyes in each of the paddocks across the property.

I was filled with sadness that we were losing Ruth and quietly glad to be here because I wanted to keep an eye on Sophie who had become one of the most important beings in my life.

We were not sure what to expect with the horses who would witness Ruth's death, in particular Sophie. I felt my throat constrict and tears well in my eyes at the thought of farewelling beautiful Ruth, accompanied by concern for my horse. Sophie had not experienced death since her mother. How would she react to what she was about to witness?

I had Sophie's halter in hand but did not want to put it on her unless she appeared likely to get in the way, which she looked she like doing when Katherine slipped a halter on Ruth. I looped Sophie's lead rope around her neck, keeping a light contact. Once Katherine had led Ruth to where we needed her to be however, Sophie relaxed and followed me at liberty when I released the lead rope from around her neck. While Sheila was gathering her supplies from the back of the land rover, Kevin, Katherine and I took a moment to say our goodbyes to the beautiful mare.

"Thank you for taking my girl under your wing, you are so special Ruth, its time to rest now," I said, gently rubbing her neck. She looked so tired. I could feel the tears starting to form in my eyes as I turned back towards Sophie who was standing close, but not in the way. Margaret and Lorna also stood, at liberty, nearby. Lorna the more sensitive of the two backed away as Sheila approached while Margaret stood half way between Ruth and Lorna. Ruth was so ill that her blood did not clot at all when Sheila injected the sedative. Shortly afterwards Ruth's head dropped a little lower as her eyelids drooped, Sheila said her own goodbye and inserted the second shot. Ruth gave a little whicker as she gently slid to the ground, which

Sophie responded to with concern, nostrils dilating and eyes wide. It was a kind and gentle passing, far different to what she would have witnessed with her own mother's death.

Lorna had moved off with Moonlight in tow as soon as Sheila had injected Ruth. Margaret stood watch as I moved towards Ruth's body, Sophie followed me, sniffing Ruth's face gently as she moved past. Sophie went to Margaret, standing at a respectful distance, obviously needing comfort and assurance from the lead mare.

Sheila checked Ruth to make sure she was definitely gone, "Better than getting your bum eaten out by dingos old girl," she quipped gruffly.

I turned back to Sophie in time to see her process, extending her tongue with strong and definite lip licking for several minutes. I had seen Sophie process like this before, many times, when experiencing a physical or energetic release during Equine Touch. I had never seen such intense processing outside a session before. I realized I was observing an authentic emotional release.

Sophie seemed to display a strong level of uncertainty about the whole event. She had seen death before, but it had been violent and ugly. This was not. Lorna had chosen to walk away as though it wasn't happening, and Margaret stood watching Ruth, Sophie, Lorna and us with a comprehension mingled with disbelief that her old companion was now gone.

Slowly we turned and headed back across the paddock, having previously agreed to allow the mares time to process Ruth's death by leaving them with her body for as long as necessary. The warmth of the day might interfere with the length of time, but having experienced equine grieving previously, when Lorna had lost a foal, we knew it was important to give the horses' time. At the gate I stopped and looked back. Sophie had commenced eating while Margaret remained exactly in the same position.

Lorna had moved in close to Ruth and was standing, head low, over her body with little Moonlight mimicking her to one side. They stood that way for half an hour. During that time Sophie and Margaret wandered over to Ruth, stood for a few minutes, and then left only to return a few minutes later, repeating the pattern several times.

I am not entirely sure how much time passed as we sat, drinking cups of tea, chatting and lapsing into comfortable silence before deciding it was time.

We headed back to the paddock. As we reached the gate I saw that Margaret and Lorna were standing like sentinels on either side of Ruth's motionless body. Margaret was baring her teeth, driving Sophie out of the 'group' and Sophie, while respectful, was obviously distressed by not being able to approach Ruth.

We haltered each of the horses and as Katherine and Kevin led Margaret and Lorna away, I led Sophie over to say that final goodbye to Ruth. It only took her a minute, one small wicker and sniff and she was ready to follow the others.

We released the horses into the big paddock and watched as they slowly moved across the distance towards the rest of the mob – one gelding and two brumby mares both with young foals at foot and Margaret's recently weaned filly.

Margaret seemed slightly disconnected as the two groups of horses merged. We watched Sophie approach Carranya and they stood, muzzle to muzzle, for several minutes. It had all the appearance Sophie telling Carranya 'all about it' and being comforted by the big bay gelding.

Sophie had responded far better to the death of Ruth than I had expected. She did not revert to the extreme withdrawn and disconnected behaviour she had exhibited as a younger horse. I was beginning to realize that Sophie's journey to emotional wholeness was also my journey to the same destination.

The emotional consistency expressed by those around her – horse and human – was proving a key element to her grounding and well being. This meant I would need to learn to accept and understand my own emotions, without judgement. Was I ready?

Photo Courtesy of Katherine Waddington. Sophie and other rescued horses following birth at Wadi Farm

Photo Courtesy of Katherine Waddington. Sophie (right) and Ruth (left)

Chapter 5

EMOTIONAL CONGRUENCE

When Sophie came into my life my world was a mess. Six months before her rescue my marriage had ended. I was trying to remember who I was and what I wanted after years of "being so mindful of what is going on around me that I had lost consciousness of self." According to Alexander Lowen MD in his book Bioenergetics, this is frequently true of hypersensitive individuals. If there was one thing I can remember being told throughout my childhood it was, "Elizabeth, don't be so sensitive!" This taught me that my emotions had no value.

Sophie arrived at a time when I had very few material possessions, a secure job but little else. I had no idea where the money would come from to pay for her. I knew that the price Sheila asked would nowhere near cover the costs of her rescue, but that did not help with the reality that I was just getting by financially.

I trusted my intuition which told me I would regret it for the rest of my life if I did not take Sophie. This was a once in a life time opportunity to have a silver brumby of my own, fulfilling a childhood dream that had been planted after reading the Silver Brumby books. How many people truly have the opportunity to live a childhood dream?

Despite my financial circumstances, I had begun to experience a new sense of contentment as I slowly developed a relationship with myself based on my true values and beliefs. I knew that somehow Sophie was to be part of my life, my future.

A large part of this process focused on emotional congruence. Sophie and I both had, in the manner relevant to our individual species, emotional issues to work through in order to be centered and find congruence and balance. In 2001 and 2002, whilst living in Sydney, I had completed a Diploma in Life Coaching. This training gave me great insights into the theoretical components of emotional development and growth. Life experiences, it seemed, were now providing the practical elements.

I had heard horse trainers speak of the need for humans to possess emotional congruence when working with horses. I had not yet heard a trainer or equestrian speak of the need for the horses to experience emotional release in order to find their own inner harmony.

During the first four years of Sophie's life we took a journey together to explore the reality that horses are sentient beings and to find therapies that assist emotionally traumatized horses.

For much of that time I was more focused on Sophie's needs and her recovery than on my own emotional journey, but slowly I began to understand so much more was occurring on this healing journey. I began to understand that for much of my adult life I had been emotionally incongruent.

I had not been honest with my own self about what I wanted from life, and this had made it impossible for me to be honest with other people. In 2006 the importance of being emotionally congruent was driven home to me when my older brother, a husband and father of two young children with a successful career in environmental health, was admitted to the Perth Clinic and diagnosed with severe clinical depression. Over the coming years he would have further diagnosis including bipolar and multiple personality disorder. In seeking to understand what he was going through I endeavoured to read as widely as possible on the subject of mental health disorders.

Whilst the brain and mental health issues are as complex and varied as humans are as individuals, there did seem to be a common thread of being self aware, internally connected and congruent in the realm of mental and emotional health and well being. I do not mean to imply that being congruent is an easy or quick fix to mental health problems but I began to see that being congruent was a way of maintaining, and therefore perhaps assisting to recover, sound mental and emotional health.

Being congruent means to be fully aware of what you are thinking and feeling. Horses respond more positively to a person who is congruent – or honest – about what is happening in their mind and body. Being congruent is also about being fully present in the moment.

Unfortunately the success I had achieved in my career was due to the complete opposite. My professional life and success was entirely outcome oriented, time efficiency, multi-tasking, goal oriented objective based achievement.

I began to realize I needed to learn new ways to connect to my emotional self, instead of taking refuge in my head and rationalizing everything. I could see that my brother and I were similar in certain ways, and this included a disconnection from our emotions.

Horses are not afraid of emotions (unlike most humans). Wild born horses in particular are especially pure in their responses and are willing to be with us, to share sensitive emotional states that exist within. There is a personal power in the knowing, owning and understanding of our own emotions. This includes giving ourselves permission to feel and express them so we can more fully understand them.

Expressing emotions – especially ones that result in tears – is often viewed as weakness. There is a growing body of evidence that points to the reality that restrained emotions can lead to energy blockages in the body which can contribute to disease.

I am sure that my journey with Sophie saved me from serious health issues. I learned to listen and acknowledge emotions, without judging them, and to give myself permission to feel. I had thought that this would lead to an emotionally fraught state of being but I discovered that it actually leads to a less reactive and a less 'emotionally driven' state of being.

My most intense experience with emotional congruence and horses occurred in 2011 six weeks after my brother had unsuccessfully attempted suicide (not for the first time).

Those weeks had taken a toll and I continued to struggle with the situation and all the repercussions of my brothers' ongoing battle with his mental health issues. I was responsible for his financial and medical affairs as well as assisting to emotionally support his young children.

In the intervening weeks I had experienced anger, shock, sorrow, sadness, and grief. These emotions continued to fluctuate inside me. I had finally managed to arrange to have a weekend at home, instead of driving back and forth to the city. I drove out to the farm to visit with Sophie and I was mindful of the fact that horses are sensitive emotive receptors. Whatever I was feeling would be reflected back to me in their behaviour and the interaction I would have with them that day. I was curious but not afraid as I walked out to the paddock. I acknowledged to myself that I honestly did not know what I was feeling, and I knew that this honesty would be enough to help me enjoy and positively interact with the horses.

I walked past Margaret, with her wild born soft, wise and gentle eyes that fixed on me as I approached. She stood slightly apart from the rest of the mob. Carranya stood to my left, down the hill a little, he is long accepted by Margaret as the mob's dominant male even though he is gelded. Carranya was born wild, up in the Kimberley. I called a greeting to them both and continued walking to the main mob which comprised Lorna, Margaret's sister, Sophie, the fillies from the last few years foaling Pearl, Rose, Chipilly, Wanda and Firefly along with Darrah, the older mare who was rescued with Sophie. As I walked toward them a sudden wave of emotion rushed out from me, so quickly I could not actually identify it.

I was barely conscious of the release before the energy bounced off the horses and returned, hitting me like a physical barrier. I was stopped dead in my tracks and felt my legs go weak and then I was on the ground sobbing.

At the same moment that I fell, the horses in front of me came galloping up. I had a moment of fear, knowing on the ground I was in a vulnerable position, but all the strength had left my muscles and I had no capacity to move.

The fear was fleeting and as it vanished I was surrounded by muzzles, the horses had dropped their heads and were nuzzling my hair, chewing, licking and pushing one another to get to me.

Margaret remained on the hill staring intently while her sister Lorna stopped alongside her. Sophie was transfixed staring at me.

After a few minutes of the fillies pushing their way in Carranya walked into the circle, commanding the respect of the youngsters who stepped ever so slightly backwards. Darrah was with him and together they dropped their heads to mine, Carranya dropped his muzzle directly in front of my face and started to breathe on me. I found myself breathing with him while Darrah gently muzzled my hair. In a few minutes my tears had dried and the fillies, now filled with their natural inquisitiveness, came nosing back in to see what was happening. Carranya gently pushed my cheek with his head, once, and then again. I still felt weak but the strength was slowly returning to my body.

Carranya nudged me more firmly as if to say, "OK that's enough now, get up." I burst out laughing and felt the release of the conflicting emotions and in their absence a growing sense of peace. As I prepared to stand, Carranya, still nuzzling my hair, pulled the hair tie out of my hair and tossed it about a metre in front of me as if to force me to my feet.

I laughed again, "Hey, I need that! Alright I am getting up." I clambered to my feet, gently touching his forehead in thanks.

Sophie, who observed and participated in the group healing session but on the outer edge, appeared to have been shocked by the episode.

She walked slowly towards me, wide eyed, and then stopped about a metre away, and dropped her head to graze, only to look up and stare again. I had the sense that her uncertainty was rooted in having experienced the freedom that follows the release of emotional energy.

I did not put her halter on, but decided to let her choose to stay

Photo Courtesy of Katherine Waddington, the Big Paddock Mob

or go. Inside me was a calmness that I had not experienced since I received the phone call six weeks earlier when I was told that my brother was, once again, in the Intensive Care Unit fighting for his life. I remember thinking at the time how random it was that when he was not conscious his body fought so hard to stay alive.

Sophie decided to stay, and stepped closer. We stood for a few minutes in silence before I started to groom her. Brushing Sophie I told her all about what was happening with my brother. The relaxing sound of her breath and warm, familiar scent was the best therapy imaginable. She turned her head towards me as I worked down her neck, where she has favourite brush and massage spots, her eyes dark pools of knowing. We stood in silent communion in the cold winter sunshine, her body warm and strong.

I was overwhelmed by the experience which, after much reflection, seemed to be a culmination of the lessons Sophie had taught me over the passage of time. Subtle shifts in perception rarely afford brilliant moments of clarity. Instead they are like the waves on the shore, softly and slowly shifting landscapes.

Sophie helped me shift my internal landscape from what I wanted to do for my horse to see what she had to offer me. There seemed to be a brilliance and clarity to what I had experienced, not just in that moment but in the passing of the years since Sophie had come to me.

Theoretical components of my life coaching training were being brought to life by my interactions with my horse. Understanding and accepting emotions became an integral element of our journey.

Photo Courtesy of Katherine Waddington, Sophie and Elizabeth Communing

Even emotions I had previously considered negative, such as anger, were re-evaluated and found to have a positive role to play in a healthy, balanced life. The irony of learning from a horse the simple truth that accepting the full range of human emotions is essential to living a full and complete life was not lost on me.

There was however little time to explore the reality that the horse I had hoped to help heal was in fact helping to heal me. Sophie's life was about to hang in the balance as our journey took us down a very different path.

Chapter 6

TUMOUR

Sophie's behaviour changed considerably during 2009. She became aggressive towards other horses, more difficult to handle and started to display stallion like behaviours even to the point of mounting other mares. We were considerably worried as her behaviour worsened and consultation with Sheila suggested a hormonal imbalance, possibly due to ovarian cysts. Following her advice we followed the protocol of an injection of oestrogen to kick start ovulation. Sophie was then allowed to run with a stallion and a small group of mares. I had contemplated Sophie having a foal and was happy to see if the protocol was successful. It was not.

I knew something was terribly wrong after a short session in the round yard, where I had been doing some liberty work with Sophie. We would often finish a session by having a short bareback ride together. This particular day I clambered up the round yard panels to slide onto her warm back and asked her to walk forward. I sensed rather then felt her bodily reaction, as she did not actually move, but conveyed to me the sense of her throwing me off her back, over her head. It was a shock, and so unlike my lovely mare that I slid off her back, walked into the house and announced that we needed to take Sophie to Harradine's for ultrasounds. Harradine's Veterinary Service was an hour away, but it was the nearest facility capable of performing ultrasounds.

Katherine, Kevin and I all travelled together, with Sophie loaded in the float and were present during the ultrasound where the vet identified the cause of the problem as being a granulosa cell tumour in her left ovary. The tumour itself appeared benign however Dr Simone Herbert commented that in ten years she had never seen an ovarian tumour so large.

The tumour measured an estimated 12cm in both depth and width but the exact size couldn't be determined. Surgery was advised and this would need to be performed in Perth.

Abdominal surgery on a horse is high risk surgery and there was a strong chance she might not survive the procedure. Simone suggested liaising with Murdoch University Veterinary Hospital immediately to make them aware of Sophie's condition and I agreed, at least the wheels would be set in motion, pending a final decision.

We drove home from Harradine's with Sophie in the float and an ominous sense resting uneasily upon us. I had a significant decision to make. I was further worried by the fact that the size of the tumour must be considerable if its parameters could not be defined on the ultrasound equipment. The risk of the tumour tearing and causing internal bleeding or further damage seemed very real and very frightening.

An acquaintance of Katherine's suggested I contact Dr Bruce Ferguson at Murdoch. Dr Ferguson was a traditional trained vet who was also trained in Chinese Veterinary Medicine and was suggested as someone who may be able to assist with alternative treatment options.

I followed this up via emails. Dr Ferguson advised that he believed Traditional Chinese Medicine in the form of herbs would significantly reduce the size of the tumour. The herbs would shrink the tumour regardless of the size and he recommended a blend of herbs called Shao Fu Zhu Yu to lower abdominal pain with or without palpable mass and to invigorate the flow of Qi and the blood. It was likely that the treatment period would be several months. Based on his experience he believed there was a 60% chance of a total cure, 30% chance of a significant reduction in size, 8% chance of growth stabilization and a 2% chance of no control of growth. He also advised that he would expect to see behaviour change in 2 weeks and ultrasonic reduction in size in 4 weeks.

I knew Dr Ferguson was a proponent of the great ancient Greek fathers of Western Medicine, Aescleipius of Thassaly view, "First the word, then the herb, lastly the knife." Theoretically I concurred, however faced with what could prove to be a life or death decision for Sophie, I struggled.

I was very interested in the non surgical option however, having observed many wild horses over the years, I was aware that wild born horses do not easily take to new or different feed. I was concerned that if I took this treatment option Sophie may well not actually eat the herbs when mixed into a feed of meadow and oaten chaff, the main feed she was given when her grazing diet was supplemented. Like most of the rescued wild horse, Sophie was kept in paddocks with sufficient pasture to meet the majority of their dietary requirements. Dr Ferguson commented that, "Most herbivores tend to eat the herbs which they require to heal," which did encourage me, however I was concerned about the implications of a large mass inside Sophie. I did not know how long the tumour had been there, or what would happen if it caused any tearing of the ovary from the simple reality of gravity. We were at least 100km from the nearest vet should anything go wrong internally while the herbs did their work.

Christmas was looming and I intuitively sensed that time was of the essence. I weighed up the information and possible timeline of recovery for Sophie should I pursue the non-surgery option, discussed both options with Katherine and Kevin and we agreed that Sophie needed to be booked in at the Murdoch University Veterinary Hospital in Perth for surgery as soon as possible. I made the call the next day and made the arrangements to transport Sophie the 300km to Perth the following week.

The day of the surgery was the longest day of my life. Sophie was scheduled as the first procedure for the day, and I was advised I would be contacted after 3pm. I was on tenterhooks waiting for a call that never came.

It was after 3pm and I returned to the hospital, sick with nervous apprehension as I approached the equine barn. I walked in to where Sophie had been stabled, only to be greeted by an empty stall. Before I could panic one of the vet students assigned to Sophie saw me and pointed me in the right direction and explained that the vet was still in surgery but would come and see me as soon as possible.

I cried when I saw Sophie, she was standing, albeit tenuously. Her liquid brown eyes were telling me a tale of confusion and bewilderment. Her body trembled and her abdomen seemed to be rolling as though her internal organs were realigning themselves. I opened the stall door and slid through, she turned her head to me and that was all the movement she could muster. Heidi, the vet student, pointed out a recent pile of manure that, while small, made us both smile.

Sophie's intestines had not been paralysed by the anaesthetic – a high risk for horses undergoing any surgery. She seemed to have lost an enormous amount of weight, her flanks incredibly sunken. I couldn't believe it was the same horse I had left earlier that day.

I stood with her for an hour, stroking her head, her sides, her ears and telling her it was all fine. During that time she looked down her left side, towards her flank, about a dozen times, clearly knowing 'something was different back there', even though she was still heavily sedated.

Finally the vet arrived. Dr David Murphy advised that he was delighted with the ease of removal, astounded by the size of the tumour and took delight in pulling the 3kg bagged organ from the fridge to show me when I queried the actual size. Everything had gone well, however the risk of complications from infection, colic type symptoms from gut related problems and the like remained high for the next 48 hours.

The morning after Sophie's surgery I returned and checked her vital statistics, noting her temperature had risen to over 39 degrees Celsius at 8pm but then had dropped back to 38 degrees Celsius by midnight. There was a lot of information on the sheet I did not understand but her heart rate, body temp and status were easy enough to follow. I sensed that if she had been going to contract an infection it would have been during that period of time when her temperature climbed.

Sophie's condition remained steady for the next few days and I began to look forward to getting her home. I also began to read Linda Kohanov's book, 'The Tao of Equus' which I had purchased whilst trying to keep my mind occupied on the day of Sophie's surgery, even though I didn't open the book that day.

The words of the book now seemed to leap out off the pages at me, resonating with my own experiences and helping me to identify that there was a construct to define what Sophie and I had shared over the years. Just as exciting was the subsequent realization that equine guided learning and therapy was a recognized modality gaining credence and incredible results around the world.

I read portions of the book aloud to Sophie who quickly grew restless in her confined stall, never having been restrained to such a small space before. I spent the next few days visiting Sophie each morning and afternoon for several hours at a time. I began to consider a future that included sharing the healing magic of horse and human interactions with other people, to help them move towards emotional wholeness.

Within a week Sophie was considered well enough to return home and her recovery from surgery was remarkable. Her discharge letter instructed she was to be kept in a stall for 30 days on returning home and that during this period of time she could be, "lead rope grazed." I explained to the vet that Sophie would be in a small foaling paddock as we did not have stables. This was approved so long as her movement was restricted. I was by now quite nervous as to the real possibility of her bursting a staple. The incision wound was 40cm long and neatly sutured internally and supported by external staples.

I need not have worried as Sophie paced her own recovery extremely well with the innate wisdom of the wild born horse.

Within three weeks she was increasingly active with small trots

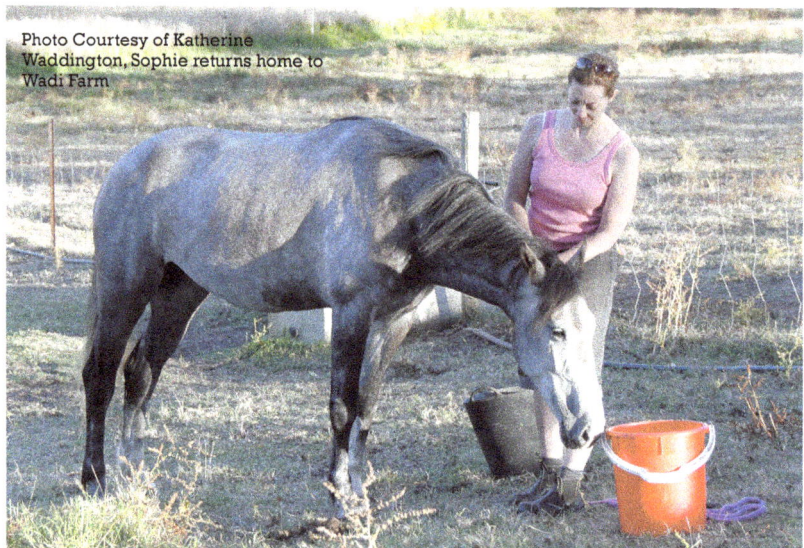

Photo Courtesy of Katherine Waddington, Sophie returns home to Wadi Farm

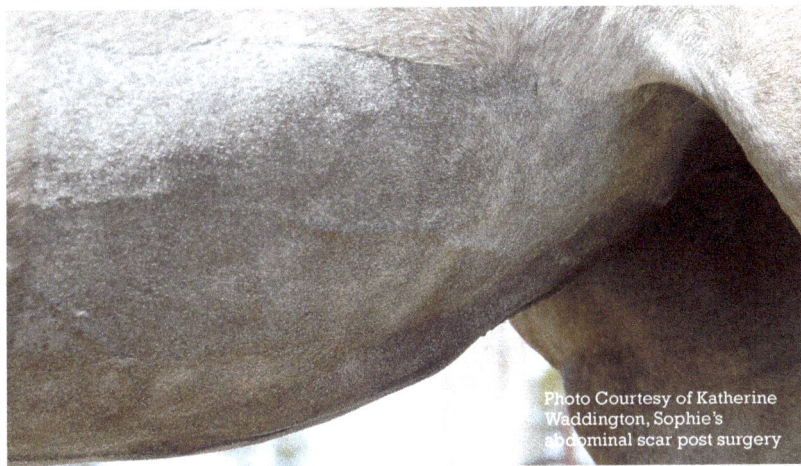

Photo Courtesy of Katherine Waddington, Sophie's abdominal scar post surgery

up and down the fence line from her favourite corner of the paddock to the water trough.

Sheila had suggested arnica and rescue remedy, both of which were being added to her morning feed. She was eating like I had not seen her eat since the first few months of her rescue. She seemed to put on weight and fill out with every mouthful. Polishing off a solid hard feed with minerals and supplements and half a bale of hay each day her body became round in a way it had not been for months. When the 41 staples were removed there was only a neat scar line with minimal scar tissue along her mid line.

During this phase of Sophie's recovery I often sat in the paddock with her, usually having a cup of tea and mulling over all that we had experienced together. The conscious realization of life lessons I had subconsciously absorbed during my time with Sophie started coming thick and fast. As a child I had always been very intuitive and I had learned to use this gift to my advantage in my professional life. My personal life was far less successful however and in observing Sophie's detachment over the years I began to see a reflection of my own self. I came to realize that I had learned to disassociate on an emotional level at an early age. The protection afforded to me by not owning my feelings safeguarded me in times of trouble, but also robbed me of the joy, the peace, the contentment and the beauty of life. Slowly, over the years since Sophie came into my life, I had begun to reconnect with my authentic self.

I started researching specific equine facilitated learning and therapy models but there seemed no opportunity to study Equine Facilitated Learning in Australia. My online search did uncover a short, powerful You Tube video of a gentleman called Franklin Levinson working with a child wearing a bright orange t-shirt and a horse called Voo. This young boy was described by his mother as suffering with, "Epilepsy, seizures, dyslexia," and being, "unable to follow instructions due to an extremely short attention span."

During his session with Franklin and Voo this young boy followed instructions with rapt attention, led the horse around the yard, stopped and backed up the horse, led the horse over a small jump, circled the horse back over the jump and concentrated the entire time. His mother was in tears seeing this amazing outcome.

I couldn't find any links between Franklin Levinson and training opportunities in equine facilitated learning. There were some exciting programs available in the USA, but most cost between $5,000 and $10,000. Sophie's vet bills had accumulated at $4,000. Even if the training options on offer had resonated with me, I lacked the financial capacity to proceed.

I considered myself fortunate that during the past year I had successfully applied for a new job in another town, nearby Bridgetown. This job, a higher level local government role in community services, would enable me to pay for the vet bills which were my immediate priority. I had left my home of 3 years in Nannup and moved to Bridgetown, while Sophie remained at her Wadi Farm home with Katherine, Kevin and the other Earaheedy horses.

The month before I was start the new job I received a telephone call from my Mum advising that my brother was in the Intensive Care

Unit at Royal Perth Hospital following a car accident in which his car and a truck had collided. It had been a difficult two years for him. His marriage had ended as he struggled with his depression and ongoing diagnosis and medication changes which seemed to create as many problems as they assisted with. Mum was distraught and I assured her I would meet her at the hospital as soon as I could safely travel the three and half hour journey to Perth.

My brother was in intensive care for 10 days in an induced coma much of the time. I was aware that some friends and family were speculating whether or not he had deliberately turned his vehicle into the oncoming truck. That he could choose to end his own life, especially with two beautiful children to live for, was beyond my capacity to comprehend.

I couldn't imagine the horror the driver of the truck, who had done no wrong, experienced. I could not reconcile my brother deliberately doing that to an innocent. What I did know was that an off duty police officer who witnessed the accident stopped, and gave my brother CPR until such time as the ambulance arrived. This was during a time frame of 45 minutes and it saved his life.

My brother was transferred from ICU in his second week of admittance and spent considerable time in hospital recovering from the accident. He had incurred injuries to the head which, along with the electro-therapy he and his former wife had agreed to when he was first diagnosed with depression, had contributed to memory loss, however his cognitive function appeared to be intact. He had no recollection of the days leading up to the accident.

After several weeks in Perth sitting around in various hospital wards it was time to head home to start my new job. I hoped that this would be a portent of good times to come as my brother's recovery appeared to be progressing slowly, but well. I was eager to get home to reconnect with Sophie, all the horses, and my life – far away from the hectic pace of the city.

Chapter 7

SOPHIE'S FUTURE

Sophie's recovery from abdominal surgery progressed well and in a quicker time frame than her post operative care notes suggested. I felt that the instinct of a wild born horse, whose primary goal is about survival, was a significant factor in her recovery. I decided to allow Sophie to pace her own recovery and trusted her not to move too much, too fast. I was still anxious something might 'go wrong' and it was not without trepidation that I observed her trotting short distances and calling for a companion horse well ahead of advised timeframes. Learning to let go and trust was still part of my journey. Within six months Sophie was fully integrated back into herd life in the big paddock mob. She adapted to 'normal life' quickly and easily. I realized there was great value in learning to take life one day at a time and to accept that while I could never control what 'might' happen I could always control how I responded to what 'did' happen.

It was during this same time period that we began to realize Sophie's knees, which had been severely compromised due to her difficult start in life, were worsening quicker than anticipated. Sophie's movement in the paddock was fine, exceptional at times and she could spin on a dime. However moving under saddle was different and Sheila advised only very light pleasure riding would be best in order to safeguard her knees and long term health and well being.

I was saddened by the realization that the long hours of riding adventures I had planned for our future would not be realized. That sadness was tempered however with gratitude for still having Sophie in my life. I had faced the prospect of potentially losing her during the past year as a result of the tumour and resultant surgery. I began to consider what the future might hold for Sophie. I had been advised that her chances of becoming pregnant were not significantly affected by the removal of one ovary and considered the possibility of her having a foal.

Sophie had made it very clear that she was not interested in helping damaged or traumatized horses as some of the other horses on the property did. This surprised me as some of the rescued horses clearly relished this role. Sophie avoided horses with trauma or emotional damage like the plague. The charity had grown in strength and numbers over the intervening years since the initial rescues on Earaheedy Station. Katherine and Kevin's property had become one of three informal rehabilitation properties where rescued horses were given time and space to adapt to a life with fences, humans and were nourished physically with food, water and a herd environment prior to commencing their taming.

I had observed that within the herd every horse had a job to perform, and this affected how the horses interacted with humans. I was perplexed by Sophie, who clearly had lead mare potential, but lacked 'street cred' due to her age, inexperience and the fact that she had never had a foal.

As she had grown, Sophie had clearly climbed up the herd hierarchy and was accepted by the matriarchs, Margaret and Lorna, as a guardian mare. This was a phrase I used to express the role of a lead mare who lives on the edge of the herd, often appearing to be alone, grazing quietly but keeping a constant eye on potential danger and what was going on with the herd. I don't know if wild herd mobs always have a guardian mare. I think it depends on the size of the herd. It was also interesting to note that the wild horses were always higher up the hierarchy than domestic horses introduced to the mob, even the lowest placed wild born horse would always be above a domestic born horse.

I had also noticed that Sophie, despite her quiet ways, was interested in people. I began to revisit my idea of pursuing a future in the world of equine facilitated learning. I read Linda Kohanov's book, The Tao of Equus again and related to her experience of owning a horse who was unable to be ridden due to a leg injury.

I revisited my Internet search and discovered an opportunity was shaping up to undertake a two week training clinic in Victoria early in 2011 with Arianna Strozzi. The training was still frightfully expensive at $5,000 but was half the price of participating in Linda Kohanov's apprenticeship program, which also required travelling to the USA. Travelling interstate and finding $5,000 was going to be enough of a time and financial challenge, but I determined to start saving and registered my interest.

I felt frustrated that things were progressing so slowly with equine facilitated learning in Australia, the training opportunities were so limited and it seemed this country was trailing behind the rest of the world in this incredible modality. I was still learning about synchronicity and learning to trust that things happen at the right time.

As the year progressed I met someone who was to become a new friend, who was breeding Percheron horses in nearby Dinninup. Lindsay Newland was a member of the charity and after chatting on Facebook we met a couple of times so I could meet her stunning stallion Kamilaroi Bombadier, with the stable name Bardi. Bardi is a beautiful, gentle stallion with great bloodlines. Sophie, being a foundational Waler carried Percheron genes and I decided to see if she was interested in producing a foal with Bardi. Lindsay was charging affordable stud fees as Bardi's foals, while impressive, were all quite young and his reputation was not yet fully established.

I believed it would only be a matter of time before his reputation resulted in an increase in stud fee, and the limited availability of pure Percheron bloodlines in the south west of WA prompted me to take advantage of the opportunity, despite my attempts to keep saving for the equine facilitated learning clinic.

The winter of 2010 was drawing to a close when plans were made to transport Sophie from Wadi Farm in East Nannup to Dinninup, approximately 65km east, for a few weeks over the spring and summer.

I was feeling quietly content with where Sophie and I were at. I did not mind if she did not fall pregnant, the agreement with Lindsay was a live foal guarantee so if we did not succeed this year there was always next year.

My female whippet Topaz was due to birth early December and I hoped that the income from a litter of pure bred whippet puppies would help contribute to the 'equine facilitated learning fund' and I was almost on my feet financially again after the vet bills from the previous year.

It was early in the spring when I received a telephone call which changed everything. Katherine and Kevin had been in Margaret River visiting Sheila after the arrival of a newly rescued mob of horses from Prenti Downs when Katherine called to tell me Lilly was for sale.

I knew Lilly had been agisted at Sheila's for the past year. My former neighbour Michelle Manners had kept Lilly at her property for the first few years after the rescue and then relocated her to Sheila's property to be in a herd environment.

I had always known if Michelle sold Lilly I would buy her. I believed Sophie and Lilly deserved to be together. I had saved almost $1500 towards my training clinic but knew in that instant the money was now going to be used to purchase Lilly instead.

I ended the telephone call with Katherine very quickly and rang Michelle to discuss the options. Katherine had told me Lilly was suffering from a serious bout of founder in her front hooves which would take a good 6 – 8 months to get right, but otherwise she was in good health. I knew Michelle had invested in having Lilly trained to saddle and I was worried that she might ask more money for Lilly than I could afford. I explained to Michelle that I could afford $2,000 which I knew was the original price paid for her as a filly. Michelle was so pleased that I wanted to purchase Lilly that we agreed on the price even though we both knew she could have sold for a higher price.

I couldn't believe that I now had two silver brumbies of my own and that Lilly was at last coming home, to join my herd.

Lilly arrived in Wadi Farm shortly before Sophie left for Dinninup, the two horses had yet another amazing reunion before I explained to them both that it was time for Sophie to leave for a few weeks, but that she would be coming home again soon.

We took Sophie to meet Bardi at the Dinninup property on a warm summer morning early in December. I could tell from the moment she came down off the float that she was not interested in Bardi. She had already cycled twice that spring so I knew she was hormonally capable of reproducing but doubted it was going to happen. She stayed with Lindsay for 3 weeks and did not cycle once in that time

Photo Courtesy of Katherine Waddington. Sophie coming in to greet Lilly

Photo Courtesy of Katherine Waddington Lilly, home at last

and so we accepted that he was not the stallion for her and took her home to spend the summer with Lilly.

Sophie seemed to have regressed a little after her time away, withdrawing into herself. I hoped that spending the warmer months back at Wadi Farm would help restore her equilibrium.

Meanwhile, Topaz had given birth to 10 puppies and my time for the remainder of that summer was spent on supporting her to care for the amazing creatures she had bought into the world. I was overwhelmed by the responsibility of finding 10 good homes for these puppies and at the same time excited by the thought of securing them suitable homes that would enable me to once again get on track financially with the now defunct savings scheme for equine facilitated learning.

Soon after Lilly came home, Katherine and Kevin were contacted by an agent for internationally acclaimed equestrian photographer, Bob Langrish.I had to confess my ignorance as to his reputation as one of the most elite international equestrian photographers in the world. Katherine, as a photographer herself, was extremely excited that Bob had requested to travel to Wadi Farm to photograph Western Australian wild born horses.

I was soon educated as to Bob's incredible 38 years of specialization in the field of equestrian photography and his 400,000 piece equestrian photographic library that was constantly expanding. Bob has completely illustrated over 100 books. His most famous works included stunning photographs of horses running free, including Arabs and Andalusions and now he wanted to add the Australian wild horses to that portfolio. It was a privilege to meet Bob and his wife Pam, also a photographer, and to observe them take stunning photographs of our horses.

After starring as models for Bob, Sophie and Lilly spent the summer simply being horses, out in the big paddock with the mob

Photo Courtesy of Bob Langrish
Sophie (Left), Lilly (Middle) and
Strawboots (Right)

Photo Courtesy of Bob Langrish
Sophie (front), Lilly (middle) and
Strawboots (rear)

while Katherine, Kevin and I worked hard to help Lilly recover from her founder with regular body work, diet supplements and corrective hoof trimming. I was beginning to understand how things work together for good when I let go of the need to control and allowed life to flow. Sophie had not allowed Bardi to mate her and I sensed that it would not be Sophie, but Lilly, who returned to Bardi next summer.

Courtesy of Bob Langrish, Sophie

Courtesy of Bob Langrish, Lilly

Chapter 8

THE JOURNEY CONTINUES

The summer months passed in a haze of hot weather and puppies. I did not spend as much time at the farm as usual due to the demands of 12 dogs in the house. Toilet training and feeding 10 puppies as they grew was a constant round of laughter, tears and chaos. I loved every minute of it and all too soon 2011 was well underway.

The times I did spend out at the farm with the horses I realized Sophie was still not right within herself and so I asked a new friend, Sietske Noble who had expertise in Bowen and Photonic Red Light Therapy to visit. I was not aware that my friend had also begun to use therapeutic grade essential oils to support her equine clients

Photo Courtesy Elizabeth Denniss
twelve hounds in the house

and when she suggested we try some oils with Sophie I agreed, even though I wasn't really sure they would work. The journey with Sophie had well and truly taught me to have an open mind. We played with all three modalities and soon, to my delight, Sophie was once again looking fully content in her eye and demeanour. I was interested to observe that she and Lilly did not spend great periods of time together, but regularly 'checked in' on each other, clearly comfortable in knowing each other was simply nearby.

The charity had conducted another rescue, this time at Juna Downs Station, during 2010. Several horses had come to Wadi Farm for their preliminary feeding up and taming down including a young bay colt who had been named Cracker. Katherine and Kevin decided to purchase him as a future stud stallion because he possessed a good combination of temperament, conformation and the heritage genetics they valued. Lilly was still recovering from founder as 2011 progressed and Sophie was introduced to Cracker and I had the sense that he may, in time, be the father of her future foal.

I started using essential oil therapies with my horses to support them with both emotional and physical issues. I explored two key modalities being the Raindrop Technique and the Emotional Clearing Technique.

I researched the properties and quality of essential oils and, like every healing modality I bought to my horses, was caught unawares by the benefits the oils had on my own health and well being. I found myself more present, grounded and connected. I also found myself being far less critical and judgemental of myself.

The more I researched the more fascinated I became and I was able to see that the essential oils and equine body work were a powerful combination. I didn't know where all this was taking me, and I found I was no longer seeking a specific outcome. It had been six years since Sophie had come into my life and the journey thus far had been about experiencing life, not arriving at a destination. This was a lesson I was only just beginning to comprehend.

Photo Courtesy of Katherine Waddington, Sophie relaxing into an essential oils session

I was also becoming excited about the forthcoming equine facilitated learning clinic scheduled for November and paid my 25% deposit by the deadline only to be advised via an email from the event organizer that several of the other participants had requested the training be postponed due to financial issues. I was both frustrated and disappointed but resigned myself to the fact that March 2012 would afford me extra time to save the balance owing on the course fees.

I had done my customary Internet search to see if there were any other opportunities for training in this field and found nothing. The event organizer, based in Australia, then decided to bring out another trainer from the USA for the November time slot. I had read her book and it did not resonate with me so I determined to wait until March 2012.

As the autumn drew to a close I had found homes for all of the puppies, and made enough money to cover half of the training costs. Unexpectedly I found myself keeping one of the puppies, the runt of the litter a small grey and white male I had dubbed 'Munty the Runty'.

He had caught me by surprise, as I never intended to keep any of the pups. He seemed determined to stay and so I found myself telling him he could stay and then regretted having named him 'Munty'. His name was then changed to 'Monty'.

Winter came early that year and I found myself being invited to speak at clinics regarding the properties of essential oils and how I had found them beneficial. I shared my stories and my research willingly, happy to share the information. I was also contacting every Equine Touch Instructor I could in both Australia and New Zealand to see if there were any Level 2 clinics being scheduled around the time I would be in Victoria in 2012 for the equine facilitated learning clinic.

The benefits of the body work Sophie had experienced, on both the physical and emotional level, had inspired me to continue training in this modality to learn more to help her, and potentially other horses, once I was a fully qualified practitioner. There had been no Equine Touch clinics conducted in Western Australia since 2008. I realized that Sophie was again touching my life, my future direction, as without her I would never have explored any of these modalities.

An Equine Touch Instructor, Janis Hobbs, based in Victoria contacted me to advise that she was planning on conducting clinics in Western Australia in 2012. Janis also advised that she would be hosting a combined Level 1 and Level 2 Equine Touch Clinic in Victoria in February 2012. The venue was a property called Tooradin Estate which, she informed me, was located about an hour's drive south east of Melbourne. I felt I had put my intentions 'out there' and accepted there was nothing more I could do except continue to enjoy my own horses.

Katherine and Kevin continued to assist with the rehabilitation of various wild born horses rescued by the charity which was now working more closely with the Department of Environment and Conservation. I had been elected president of the charity during 2010.

I had not planned on nominating but when the inaugural president stepped down there was no other nomination from the committee. I knew the work of the charity was important and renominated for the role in 2011 when again there was no other nomination.

There was a steady stream of visitors to Wadi Farm during 2010 and 2011. People came to visit the wild brumbies, enthralled by the majesty, beauty and power of these amazing animals. Katherine and Kevin were continuing to breed quality Waler horses from foundation stock and also hosted veterinary students through the Murdoch Veterinary Hospital Extramural Farm Experience Program.

It was interesting to observe the therapeutic effect of the horses on the vet students during their practical placement. The horses clearly had both an individual and collective capacity to draw people out and help them to identify and address personal issues, problems and challenges. This was not part of placement, it just happened and over the years we began to accept there would often be a journey of self discovery for the vet students and other visitors who came to stay.

I also noticed how just being with the horses helped my niece and nephew share what was going on for them in relation to their father's mental health problems. Whenever they visited with me I always made a point of having them 'help' me with caring for the dogs and horses. This often included grooming and while I brushed one side of the horse, they would work on the other side.

The greatest moments of sharing and contemplation during their visits were always during these times. There seemed to be something about being outside, in the beauty of the natural world, with the horses, that slowed us all down and enhanced our ability to communicate collectively.

The year was passing quickly and as winter drew to a close I was growing excited about the forthcoming trip to Victoria for the long awaited equine facilitated learning training program. Early in the spring I received advice from the event organizer that because many of the individuals who had planned on attending the March 2012 clinic had in fact attended the November 2011 clinic it was looking unlikely that Arianna Strozzi would be coming to Australia in 2012. I was flabbergasted. The date had been delayed to enable people extra time to save the dollars and now it wasn't happening?

Arianna then contacted me to apologise and explain that it was simply not worthwhile for her to travel such a great distance for only a few students, which was understandable. She offered me a discount on attending the training at her ranch in California but the additional cost and time impost made the offer unviable.

I started my Internet search all over again, feeling quite dejected and downhearted. I really believed in pursuing this path, I just didn't know how to do so when it seemed at every turn the path was blocked by forces beyond my control.

This time however the Internet search bought some unexpected results. There was now an Australian Equine Facilitated Learning Association, offering a 4 day Level 1 Facilitator Clinic in Victoria for the affordable sum of $750! I read their website avidly, amazed

Photo Courtesy of Katherine Waddington, Sophie and my niece Annabelle sharing a special moment

and delighted to read that Franklin Levinson was the patron of this association.

Franklin Levinson, the very man whose work in the field of equine facilitated learning had first inspired me. I contacted the Association immediately and was advised the next clinic would be in February 2012 and was to be held at Tooradin Estate, the exact same venue as the Equine Touch training. There was a two day break between the two clinics.

I simply couldn't believe the synchronicity at work in my life. The airfares, clinic fees and accommodation were less than half the price of the original clinic. I felt like I was on my way… I didn't know to where but the door had opened and I was walking through it – or was that Sophie pushing her muzzle into my back, thrusting me through it?

Chapter 9

AT LAST

February 2012 arrived all too quickly and I was nervous about the trip to Victoria. I had no idea what to expect in the training and I was physically and mentally exhausted. My brother had been through another rough patch and suicide attempt and my young puppy had been diagnosed with an autoimmune disease. He required extra care and attention which was disrupting the pack hierarchy. Two of the other dogs had engaged in two vicious fights as they attempted to resolve who was top dog. I had called in a canine behavioural specialist to help. Mum was coming to house and dog sit for me while I took the time to travel and I was worried another fight would occur in my absence.

I drove up to Perth the evening before my flight feeling very out of sorts and realized it had been about ten years since I had actually left the state. My decision to move to the south west corner of Western Australia was based on a great love for the natural beauty of the area and I had never felt the urge to holiday anywhere else in the intervening years.

Travelling to Victoria was something I had done regularly as a teenager and in my early 20's and the familiarity of the journey returned. It was exciting to be going somewhere new. I left the Tullamarine airport in my rental car and realized I did not have the address of where I was going. I remembered the property was Tooradin Estate and determined to simply head to Tooradin and find someone local to ask for directions. That's how we do things in the country.

I arrived in the hamlet of Tooradin and was delighted with the friendly atmosphere and look of the place, the proximity to Western Port Bay gave a seaside feel which I loved.

The friendliness was not as forthcoming when I decided to ask at the Post Office for directions to Tooradin Estate. The man behind the counter advised me curtly it was not called Tooradin Estate but was in fact Lyons Estate. I mused on this for a moment, considering the Australian Equine Facilitated Learning Association website clearly stated the clinic was to be held at Tooradin Estate in Tooradin.

I determined I was in the right place and when he offered no further advice I repeated my request for directions to Lyons Estate. He begrudgingly gave me the directions, which I followed and found myself a few minutes later at the driveway to the property with the large sign stating I had arrived at Tooradin Estate. I gave a sigh of relief and realized that my encounter with the post office worker seemed symbolic of the hurdles I had faced over the years in finding somewhere to study equine facilitated learning. I was grateful I could appreciate the humour of the encounter and felt like I could relax – I had finally arrived!

I drove up the driveway towards the house looking around in amazement. I did not know what to expect, but this was certainly not it. The property was amazing; the kind of place a horse mad child would dream and draw pictures of. Green, grassy paddocks, wooden post and railing paddocks, stables, a large sandy riding arena and the house itself was regal yet inviting. There was a small group of people outside the house on the lawn as I parked the car and clambered out. A little blonde woman in RM Williams jeans and shirt came over to greet me. "Hello, I'm Sally," she said as we shook hands.

I had emailed Sally Francis, one of the owners of Tooradin Estate, to book my accommodation and had asked for a room on my own. I did not know how I would travel emotionally during the clinic and having lived on my own for ten years I felt the need for space might be important.

I felt like I was being demanding in making this request and was sure she would consider me a high maintenance visitor but my journey with Sophie had also taught me to honour and voice my own needs. I had also asked if I could arrive a day early to settle in and an extra two days between the equine facilitated learning and equine touch clinics. Sally's emails had been short, advising me, "That should be alright."

Sally was busy in the main arena with riding clients most of the afternoon but showed me to my room which was located at the far end of a long corridor. It was a stunning room, high ceilings, chandelier, ornate mahogany furniture and beautiful views of the ancient pine trees that traversed the fence line between the house and front paddock. I realized that other than Sally's room it was the only single room in the house. Two other guest rooms each contained three single beds and then there were the shearing quarters outside the main house which were also shared rooms. Sally commented that most of the equine facilitated learning clinic participants would be accommodated in the house and that I was the only person staying for the second clinic as the other participants were all local.

Horses, Heartache & Healing

Photo Courtesy of Elizabeth Denniss
Tooradin Estate Homestead

Photo Courtesy of Elizabeth Denniss
Tooradin Estate Main Arena

I thought to myself if I owned such a beautiful place I would not be able to share it with the carefree graciousness Sally possessed. Before leaving to return to her clients Sally introduced me to Hadas Sudri, a beautiful young lady from Israel who was travelling ahead of her husband. They hoped to find work and stay in Australia once he arrived and she was staying at Sally's to help out during the clinic.

Hadas had a list of chores to do that afternoon and I helped with the grooming of horses, fascinated to hear of her life in Israel where she had studied a 3 year degree in the field of Equine Facilitated Therapy. I had not realized such a study option existed. After quizzing her on the content of her studies I decided to leave her to the rest of her chores. I headed back into Tooradin to purchase some groceries and spent the afternoon sitting on the lawn with Sally's dogs Coco and Ruby keeping me company.

I observed the comings and goings of the property and began to adjust to the flow of life here. Everything was open and inviting and there seemed to be a natural order and flow to things without any real order or schedule. It fascinated me.

As the afternoon passed by more clinic participants arrived and I was amazed at the sense of unity and acceptance that existed as we began to come together as a group. It was my first experience in a nurturing, respectful group environment.

Everyone was on their own individual journey and yet willingly sharing a collective journey with strangers. A journey that essentially revolved around the role horses played in our lives. It was empowering and quite an eye opener for me.

The afternoon flowed into the evening as we got to know each other over a trip into town for more groceries, bottles of wine and the preparation of dinner. Sally returned to the house after her last client to find dinner well on the way to being prepared and a group of people in her home as comfortable in it as she was.

We spent the evening around the extremely large dining table, laden with food and wine and as we were all intrigued by the place Sally told us a little of it, and her family, history.

Tooradin Estate is a 400 acre property situated in South Gippsland. It was built as a sheep and cattle grazing farm in 1880.

Sally's family purchased the property in 1966 to develop their riding school business. The family conducted the first riding camp in 1967 with around 25 people staying in the house and former shearer's quarters. This began a tradition of holiday camps held on long weekends and during school holidays.

Sally's mother Judy Francis assisted clients to prepare for the show ring, dressage, showjumping, eventing and games events. She also trained many riding instructors at all levels and in a wide range of equestrian disciplines. In 2000 she received an Australian Sports Commission coaching medal from the then Prime Minister Mr. John Howard. Judy passed away in 2009.

Sally's father Derry Francis was a renowned polo player who lived nearby and visited Tooradin each day. We were all impressed with his courteous manners and enjoyed his pleasant company over a cup of tea on the breaks or a glass of wine at dinner.

I have never, and doubt I ever will again, visit a property like Tooradin. We were all amazed by the various activities that were centered around the estate including two pony clubs, an adult riding club as well as equine facilitated learning and riding develops ability activities. Horse owners agisted their horses at the property and equestrians travelled, with their horses, to train or have lessons in the arena with Sally, or access the impressive cross country course.

Over the coming days we learned a little more about Sally, not from her directly but through Derry, Elaine Hughes and Cathy Prior, her Australia Equine Facilitated Learning colleagues. Sally became the State Coach of Rideability Victoria (formerly known as RDA Victoria), was a national coach educator and assessor for Riding Develops Ability Australia and Pony Club Australia.

She became involved in the Australian Para Equestrian teams in 1994 when she went to the World Championships in Hartpury UK as a team participant carer and then in 1996 she was appointed as Chef d'equipe of the Australian team that went to Atlanta. When Sydney hosted the Olympic Games in 2000, Sally was one of the National Technical Officials that officiated at the Para Equestrian events.

Sally was keen to return to the Australian Paralympic Equestrian team and she was appointed assistant coach for the Hong Kong team in 2008. Sally has been a part of the Equestrian Australia High Performance Program since 2009 as the Chef d'equipe of the Para equestrian team. I had also been involved in the Sydney Olympic Games as a media liaison officer for basketball and knew first hand how exciting it is to be involved in a sport you love at the Olympic level.

I think we were all a little bit in awe of Sally and felt even more privileged to be sharing the EFL experience at a place with such an amazing family and equine history.

That first night at Tooradin however we knew none of Sally's achievements, and I think that was just the way she liked it. The evening ended with everyone heading off to bed feeling relaxed and curious about what the next day would bring.

I climbed into bed that night feeling an unusual sense of peace. I wasn't worried about my dogs, or horses, or what the future held. I was simply in the present moment, enjoying where I was, who I was with, and what I was doing.

I realized that this was the way of the horse. I thought about Sophie, and the horses back home who do not worry, fret or have ongoing anxiety. If something worrisome looms on the horizon it is directly acknowledged, its implication assessed and a determined response made.

That response is made and expressed as a whole of being experience. I contemplated the difference in how I process stress and anxiety. In the first instance I would proceed through a logical, conscious mind assessment of the problem, the purpose of which was to fix the problem, reducing the stress by removing the cause. Once an appropriate course of action was identified there was no consideration for the impact the stress or problem had on my physiological body. I considered that my recent diagnosis of an overactive thyroid had links to the way in which I dealt with and processed stress, anxiety and my emotions in general.

I decided that for the next four days I would simply focus on being in the moment and enjoying the energy and personalities of those around me; to soak up the knowledge on offer and allow it to simply be an experience without judgement or analytical assessment. I felt ready, even though I did not know for what.

Photo Courtesy of Elizabeth Denniss
misty morning at Tooradin

99

Chapter 10

GETTING EDUCATED

Bright and early the next morning the house was overflowing with people all gathering around the impressively large dining table where we had enjoyed dinner the evening before. The group was now about 20 strong and other than the Australian Equine Facilitated Learning instructors Cathy and Elaine who, like Sally, were conspicuous in their branded t-shirts, nobody was quite sure who was there to participate and who was there to help out.

What particularly impressed me about Cathy and Elaine was their down to earth style. Like Sally, they did not feel the need to espouse their experience as is often the case with instructors in many equine disciplines. They each gave a brief overview of their background and why they had formed the Australian Equine Facilitated Learning Association. Essentially they believed in the value of the modality to produce long term, positive change in people's lives and wanted an association to provide some degree of professional standards in Australia.

Whilst still living in the UK, Elaine had trained with many of the original Parelli instructors and other international experts from differing horsemanship disciplines to gain a wide cross section of skills and expertise. She was reluctant to become identified with just one training method and had met Franklin Levinson years ago when she was investigating ways of bringing horses and children together in a mutually beneficial way. She saw the benefits in the therapy side of interaction with horses that did not 'use' the horse as a tool in the process, but as an active participant. Elaine became Franklin's co-ordinator in the UK until she moved to Australia in 2009.

Cathy's first horse was a gelding called Tuff on whom she learned trick riding, imitating an uncle who was a professional trick rider. Tuff was her best friend growing up especially during times when Cathy had no one else to turn to. It was during this period that Cathy first felt the benefits of EFL, before even having a name for it.

Cathy understood the power of the relationship that can develop between a horse and young person. Cathy went on to study Psychology, Counselling, Group Work, Community Services, and Disability and has been working in the disability sector for over ten years. A chance encounter with Franklin saw her become his Australian co-ordinator after training with him and then partnering with Elaine on her arrival in Australia.

I had not expected Franklin Levinson to be present during the clinic, as he and his wife live in Greece, but I was delighted when the first session kicked off with a viewing of the exact same video footage of Franklin I had found on the Internet so many years earlier. It was soul affirming.

The enthusiasm and excitement in the room was palpable over the four days. The training consisted of the clinical background to EFL, basic horsemanship skills, assessing potential therapy horses, the components of a session, challenging behaviours, legal, health and safety requirements. The 4 days were inspiring and challenging. The evenings were full of laughter and the ebb and flow of a house of women who could make things happen effortlessly. I had never felt so at home with a group of new friends, in a new environment.

Cathy and Elaine delivered the training in a Punch and Judy Show style, with Sally and her dog Ruby providing moments of abstract hilarity at the most inopportune, and therefore magically appropriate moments.

On the second day, half way through the morning theory session, Ruby stood in front of me as I sat in an antique oak and velvet chair barking at me. I thought she wanted to play and when I looked across the room at Sally the amusement twinkling in her eyes as I tried to control her dog almost had me bursting out loud with laughter. I realized that Ruby did not want to play, she simply wanted me out of her favourite chair.

I am pretty sure if she could have spoken it would have been something like, "Get out of my chair, bitch!"

The style of training was very different to anything I had experienced before and I realized that this was because equine facilitated learning is not outcome focused and therefore the training itself in many ways needed to reflect this. The sense of being able to play and be creative was essential to learning how to be a great facilitator. The day we did role model training I had the epiphany that the magic of equine facilitated learning occurred in the interaction between the client and the horse, not in the activities or lesson plan. The same qualities that are vital to being a good horse trainer came into play – having flexible boundaries, mental focus, emotional congruence, creative visualization and clarity of intent were key ingredients. This is what would give a client a good experience, because it allowed the creation of a safe place for whatever needed to happen, to happen.

The training ended all too soon and we were saying our goodbyes. The house seemed suddenly quiet when everyone had left and Sally headed out for dinner with family. I took my book down with me to the estuary to read whilst enjoying fish and chips.

I didn't open the book, but sat on the grass watching the light dance on the water and thinking, with gratitude, of Sophie and how without her in my life I would not have met the amazing people I had just spent the past few days with or be on the brink of something so new and exciting. I spent the evening in solitude, mulling over all I had learned during the clinic and how it bought so much depth and clarity to my own personal experiences.

Horses are now recognized for their ability to transport humans to higher levels of emotional, spiritual and mental awareness. Experience with Sophie had taught me that emotional congruence is a vital element in connecting with horses.

Being in an emotionally incongruent state gives off a different energy vibration to a person who is emotional congruent. Humans have the same capacity to sense incongruity as horses, we just don't develop or use the sense. Perhaps it is an unfortunate by-product of a society so far removed from nature, that by and large we are encouraged to dismiss our 'gut feelings' or 'sixth sense' as illogical. My time with Sophie helped me to develop an authentic, intuitive sense which had led me here to Tooradin, to the realm of equine facilitated learning.

The horses I had been privileged to meet and work with during the training clinic, including the remarkable Tuff, reinforced what Sophie had already taught me. Horses prefer it when I am not hiding any agendas, intentions or even unconscious emotions such as

Photos Courtesy of Dianne Robertson
Elizabeth working with William to refine
horsemanship skills at Tooradin Estate

Photos Courtesy of Dianne Robertson
Elizabeth working with William to refine
horsemanship skills at Tooradin Estate

sadness, anger, frustration or fear. I create confusion for them when I project one thought or intention but hold a different (often opposite) feeling in my body.

I realized that Sophie is most willing to connect with me when I am open, relaxed, receptive and free from perceptions about desired outcomes and expectations.

It is a waste of time and energy to try and project happiness when I am feeling frustrated, sad or angry. Sophie doesn't care about who I am trying to impress or what I am pretending to feel, be or do – she sensed who I was even when I had forgotten myself.

It was quite a unique experience, to meet and work with new horses that I had no connection or history with. During the training clinic, many of us would take time during the breaks to wander out and simply be in the paddocks with just the horses for company. We did not discuss what occurred during those times, with each other, we just knew it was part of the experience, the individual journey.

I observed the power of possibility when people are willing to listen in their interactions with horses. These people, like me, believe that the power of the horse is not in being our beasts of burden, but in facilitating a connection that generates reflection, healing and empowerment.

I pondered the possibilities that might exist if I could carry home with me an ability to put aside my agendas and objectives; to stop focusing on what I wanted to achieve, and just experienced life as a way of being.

Chapter 11

LIFE LESSONS FROM WATCHING WILD HORSES

In the solitude of the evening, after the energetic, inspiring and lively exchanges of the past few days, I reflected on many of the conversations I had with my new found friends and kindred spirits. I sipped a cold beer and enjoyed the fish and chips I had purchased.

Many of my new friends had been intrigued to hear about the experiences of working with wild born horses, and the rescues of the charity. In small groups we had lengthy discussions about the fabric of Australian culture, and how the brumby was an indelible part of the nation's history. I realized that in watching wild horses over the past six years, I had gleaned insights that were proving invaluable to my education and experience in the world of equine facilitated learning. One key element of this was communication, horse style.

Horses sense the energy that surrounds them all the time – their very survival depends upon it – they process information predominantly via energy awareness of sensations in their bodies. This is especially true of wild born horses who retain an acute fight-or-flight response to any potential threat.

Humans, on the other hand, have become much more adept at rationalization and therefore we do not always listen to what our emotions and body resonance is conveying. This can often lead us into dangerous, or less than ideal, circumstances in how we are living. Instead of focusing on a specific outcome in my interactions with horses, I had learned to take my cues from Sophie, centering myself and asking, "What is most important in this moment?"

I had to learn to stop expecting perfection from both of us. Perfection is simply not appropriate in most instances because it is impossible, yet too often I would strive and fail and then beat myself up over the inevitable failure. This lesson gave me greater freedom and peace in my work and other areas of my life. I noticed that humans strive so hard to achieve the impossible and in so doing lose the precious gift of what is.

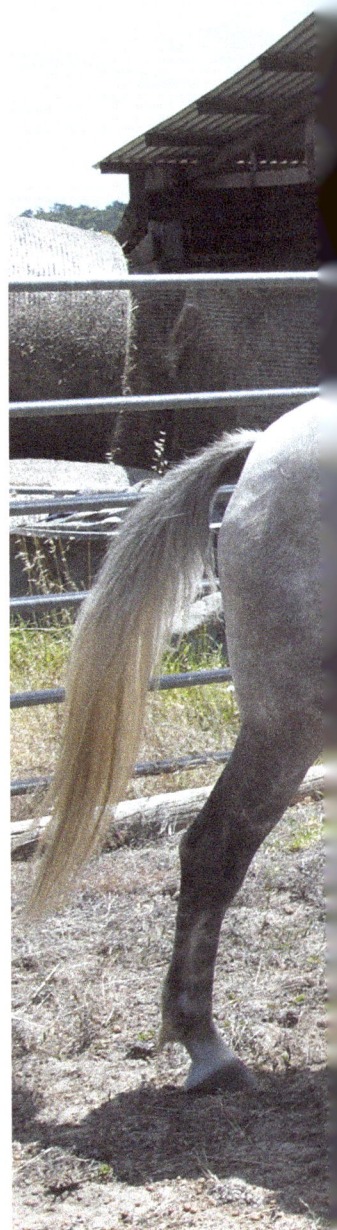

Photo Courtesy of
Katherine Waddington
Elizabeth and Sophie

I don't know if horses are spirit guides, but I do know that Sophie, simply by being a horse, responds to the quality of my emotional energy. I cannot manipulate her. Every time I tried to make things 'right' or control the situation and outcome I was left bewildered, frustrated and exhausted. This was replicated in my life outside the paddock too.

Learning to let go and move into a place of trust, accepting that what emerged naturally would be sufficient was another gift that came with the gradual passing of time as I strove to 'help Sophie'.

Sophie responded to the release of old energy, both hers and mine. Probably because horses have little desire to be physically close to individuals who are not fully present, in their bodies. This was also a gift of understanding. The main method of equine communication involves horses communicating with each other through their bodies – what they sense and feel in their environment is transmitted energetically to each other. Watching a group of horses respond simultaneously to a perceived threat is evidence of this phenomenon.

Sophie taught me body-centered awareness is the most natural approach to life, the most natural 'way of being'. In so doing I began to learn the art of becoming fully aware of myself as a primary step in removing the stress and tension I unconsciously carry. I learned that it is OK to be uncomfortable within myself, the important part is knowing I am uncomfortable and allowing it to be and trusting that it will pass and I will be OK when it does.

In observing the differences between humans and horses, I realized that it is rare to find a human be-ing. We are so busy do-ing – chasing life – to simply stop, and be.

Humans, it seems, are driven by a desire to control others and circumstances to feel safe, but that safety is an illusion.

Watching Sophie I began to realize how little she did – she simply lives in a powerful, authentic, state of being – connected with the natural environment and her surrounds. When I am completely honest with Sophie about what I am feeling and experiencing I immediately experience a strong sense of peace and relaxation.

Sharing these reflections with my new friends and equine facilitated learning colleagues clarified a number of my own experiences. I often found myself thinking back to that day in the round yard when my horse had communicated to me, in a way I still do not fully understand, how much pain she was in.

How had that occurred? Sophie did not move a single hoof, or make any untoward movement at all, yet I knew that to ask her for even a single step forward was causing her great pain.

With the gift of hindsight and an understanding of the natural law of gravity, a 3kg tumour in an ovary would certainly have been painful, especially with me sitting on her back.

I began to realize that horses communicate with great clarity, without the use of spoken language, via gesturing, posturing and when absolutely necessary, sound. They express their needs, wishes and emotions to each other and to the humans who choose to listen. The way horses communicate demonstrates an awareness that is lacking in human interactions.

I compared horse communication to how humans interact and began to wonder if humans have become overly dependent on words which can often contradict the unspoken 'body language' that is occurring in an exchange. Even in instances where we are not seeking to deliberately deceive, if our emotions are not congruent and if we are not operating from a place that supports our values and beliefs, our body language may well contradict the words we are using. It is no wonder we so often misunderstand one another.

Horses have the capacity to assess what is going on at an internal, emotional and completely un-intellectual level. Humans, on the other hand, over intellectualize and interpret information through filters created by personal experience. In seeking to find a point of reference for the information being relayed, misconceptions arise due to our inability to stop analysing what we are hearing and instead simply listen in order to understand.

I began to observe human interactions more closely and realized that it is a quirk of human nature that we seem to need to determine whether we agree or disagree with everything that is presented to us. Perhaps this is the ego needing to equate everything to 'self' rather than acknowledge 'other' and in so doing we fail to listen empathetically because we feel challenged, and therefore threatened.

In comparison, it became evident that horses communicate by addressing each issue, in the moment and then simply moving on. I resolved to try to emulate this one element of communication – to possess the confidence and ability to voice individual needs honestly, in any given moment, without judgement.

Horses communicate with a level of respect that involves both hearing and listening to the needs being expressed by individual herd members. Releasing totally any personal judgement in relation to my own needs, and the needs of others, was a priceless gift bestowed by Sophie as we travelled through life together.

I can see now that humans often fall into the trap of either talking, or listening, too much and both can have negative impact on the quality of life. When we concentrate too much on communicating what we have to say, we lose the capacity to listen, care for and support others. When we concentrate too much on listening to what others have to say we lose the capacity to listen, care for and support ourselves.

Horses are social creatures that live in a hierarchal herd system. Each horse knows his or her place and their role within the collective group.

A solitary horse cannot survive in the wild as horses need each other to share the responsibility of finding food and water. A wild mob also depends on other herd members to be on the alert for danger, this allows times of rest for all herd members.

A wild mob of horses will have a stallion whose job is to protect the mob and a lead mare whose job is to guide the mob to safety, food and water and to ensure protocols are met within the group dynamic.

Depending on the size of the mob there may also be guardian mares who are somewhat dominant but whose role is to be 'on the edge' of the mob and who will often alert the lead mare to imminent danger so she can decide how to respond to the threat. Each member of the mob has a role to play and knows their individual responsibility to the rest of the family. In considering the role of effective communication in a herd environment, I realized that while humans are social creatures we now live in a civilization that devalues the importance of community and family, or worse still allows corrupt forms of tribal values to negatively influence individuals.

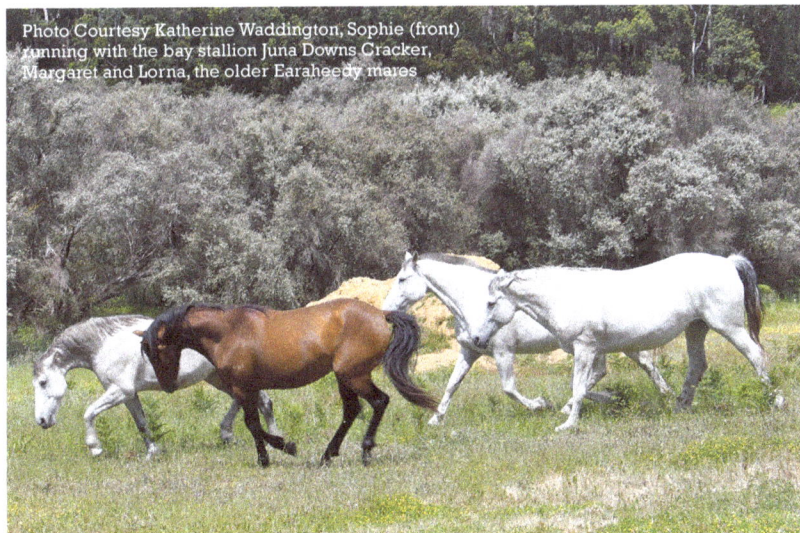

Photo Courtesy Katherine Waddington, Sophie (front) running with the bay stallion Juna Downs Cracker, Margaret and Lorna, the older Earaheedy mares

Intellectually we seem to understand the importance of community, of family and contributing but our society still values material possessions, the accumulation of wealth, power, consumerism and prestige above all else.

In a herd, horses identify and maintain their role in the group for the overall good of the collective. Horses continually negotiate their roles to ensure the best quality of leadership is in place because this is vital to their survival. The level of negotiation can range from subtle cues, such as a slight flattening of the ears to exaggerated displays of assertiveness such as biting and kicking. These actions are, however, always direct and to the point. In establishing their herd hierarchy horses do not seek to overpower or humiliate other members of the herd.

Horses enforce their assertive nature only long enough to establish a clear line of communication. They do not abuse their ability to influence other herd members.

I could not help but contrast this to humans, who do not always exhibit the same level of respect and who often exert a lot of energy attempting to influence others.

Conflicts within wild horse mobs are quickly resolved to ensure energy is conserved so that when danger or challenge presents the mob has the individual and collective energy to deal with it. It is the clear, direct and easily understood communication amongst the horses that allows this to occur. Unity is essential for survival.

The lessons I had learned regarding the need for emotional congruence suddenly became a foundation for so much more knowledge. Being congruent was suddenly less about 'me' – it was now about communicating and connecting with others (humans and horses) in an authentic manner that fostered both giving and receiving.

I cannot say that I understand how Sophie conveyed her pain and discomfort to me via a visual image in my brain and a physical sensation in my body that day in the round yard. I do know one thing, that it was the quality of our relationship that enabled her to share vital information with me which was essential to her survival. I was glad she had taught to me listen to unspoken communication.

As I sat, eating my fish and chips by the estuary I realized that the unique atmosphere and bonding that I had been privileged to share during the clinic was in fact an experience of the horse herd dynamic. It was a mind blowing realization and precious gift that, with the passing of time, would prove to be cherished by many of us who were there to experience it.

Photo Courtesy of Katherine Waddington, wild born horse herd at Wadi Farm

Chapter 12

COMING HOME

I stayed another week in Victoria. Sally kindly allowed me to stay for the two days break in between the Equine Facilitated Learning Level 1 Clinic and the Level 2 Equine Touch Body Work Clinic, also held at Tooradin. I had expected to spend the time alone, which would have been a nice respite. However Sally offered to have me tag along to various clinics she was either presenting or attending so the two days were full and exciting. It had been four years since I studied my Equine Touch Level 1 and I was a bit rusty in the technique. Janis Hobbs, the Australian Co-ordinator for Equine Touch soon had me refining my breathing and the body work technique. Before I knew it I was boarding the plane home after the best holiday I had ever experienced.

I knew it would be difficult to get back into the routine at home, I was so fired up with my equine pursuits that returning to my job in local government would be somewhat of a let down. I was very much looking forward to seeing my dogs and horses, all of whom I had missed dreadfully.

On the flight home I pondered further where the equine facilitated learning journey might take me. I couldn't see where or how it would fit into my life, but then six years earlier I hadn't known how a young, wild born filly would fit into my life either. I reminded myself that these things have a way of working themselves out. Within a week of returning home, one of my work based committees the Disability Access and Inclusion Committee identified a forthcoming funding opportunity that would provide up to $50,000 funding to deliver programs aimed at assisting people with disabilities, and their families, participate more fully in existing community or sporting clubs.

At a committee meeting we discussed different program options. Two of the committee members were representatives from local disability support service providers. They both advised that a number of their clients had expressed interest in a horse related program. There was no Riding Develops Ability program in the local area.

I sat in the meeting quietly for a few minutes, absorbing that information and gathering my thoughts. None of the committee members knew of my interest in equine facilitated learning or the fact that I had just returned from the training. Finally, I spoke up and offered a very brief abstract about the possibility of an equine facilitated learning program, what it might look like and how it might operate. Their response was enthusiastic.

I was encouraged to make contact with the funding body and if the proposal met with their approval to proceed with a formal application. My mind was reeling. I had only just completed my Level 1 training. Could I actually do this? There was a lot of planning involved, and I knew that there was no previous model I could base a program on that suited the requirements of the funding body.

I made contact with the local representative from the Disability Services Commission who was less enthusiastic about the concept. She advised me it would not be funded because it was a new program, not an existing program. I double checked the guidelines and there was no reference to such an exclusion, the key was linking the program to an existing sporting or community club. I proceeded to speak with representatives from the local horse and pony club, who were very receptive to the concept. I commenced working on the application and submitted the document by the deadline

It was an unusual application, because the program allowed for a six month planning phase once funding was approved.

I knew this was both unusual and critical for the program to be successful. A week after the application was submitted my boss asked me if I would be interested in attending training in Project Management. The training was being funded by the Local Government Manager's Association. Due to recognition of work place experience and learning, we would attend two full days of lectures and then complete a comprehensive project management planning assignment.

I saw this as the best opportunity to progress the planning phase of the equine facilitated learning program and achieve an additional diploma at the same time. One week before attending the training I was advised that the funding application had been successful to the value of $49,500.

Once the funding was received a steering group was established to oversee the implementation of the program and refine the project management plan I had prepared. The program began to take on a life of its own.

The grant provided funding for 4 scholarships for the clinician fees to train local people as Level 1 Facilitators with Australian Equine Facilitated Learning. There was sufficient additional interest in the training that instead of sending the successful scholarship candidates to Victoria for the training, we were able to bring Franklin, Elaine and Sally to Western Australia to conduct a clinic in 2013.

Two weeks before they came to deliver the clinic I attended my Level 2 training with them back at Tooradin where I was reunited with many of the amazing women who had participated in the Level 1 training. I was excited beyond measure to meet Franklin, and very impressed with his gentleness and genuine interest in both people and horses.

Franklin has been a professional horseman for nearly 50 years and he inspired me with his personal goal that the horse and human become partners and that the horse be honoured and highly respected within any horse-human activity. He created The Maui Horse Whisperer experience, the first Equine Facilitated Learning program in the Pacific Basin and one of the first in the USA. He is credited as being the first person to introduce equine facilitated learning for children with a learning disability to the United Kingdom and the first person to bring equine facilitated learning to Australia.

There were ten participants in the Level 1 training in the south-west of Western Australia in February 2013. There was a separate Level 1 clinic held in Perth. I was delighted to see so much interest in the modality and to be a part of bringing it to Western Australia.

Four of the individuals on the steering group participated in the training, including a teacher from Manjimup Senior High School, Rowan Pritchard. Rowan went on to introduce an equine facilitated learning program at the school which is growing in strength in the main stream education environment.

The four scholarship candidates were required to volunteer as facilitators in the funded program for 18 months. The three steering group members who paid for their own training also volunteered as facilitators. Like the women I had met in Tooradin, these ladies had all experienced their own version of equine facilitated therapy in their personal lives, and knew first hand the healing and positive impact horses can offer humans.

I felt privileged to observe the delivery of the training and to assist Franklin, Elaine and Sally. The training days were long and participants were able to put their boots up at the end of the day but the evenings were just as busy for the trainers. They would assess, review and discuss the progress of the participants and plan the next day's activities over dinner each evening. I would usually sit and listen during these conversations, making the most of the good company and wealth of knowledge. On the second evening, when we were discussing just how much work was involved in conducting the clinics, Elaine excused herself from dinner to take a call from Cathy, who was working her day job and had been unable to travel. Elaine returned to the table a short while later and the conversation resumed.

"Well that's official then," she stated decisively in her pommy accent as the conversation lulled. Franklin and Sally nodded so I nodded too, extremely tired after another long, hot day. "The sooner we get you trained as a trainer, the better." I kept nodding as her words sunk in, then my head shot up and realized she was talking to me.

"Me?" I said, caught completely by surprise. Everyone laughed and Elaine reiterated "Yes, you! I just spoke with Cathy and she is in agreement." Franklin looked at me and smiled and said, "We would be happy to have you on board."

The conversation then turned to the music playing in the restaurant where we were dining, and I was left wondering what had just happened.

I discussed it with Franklin again the next morning as we drove to the Warren Equestrian Centre for the final day of training. He reaffirmed that in whatever capacity I was keen to contribute they would be keen to have me. Sally also reaffirmed this at the morning tea break, telling me she had figured on it happening from the first clinic I attended at Tooradin.

I took a few moments for myself at the lunch break to absorb it all. In less than a year I had completed my Level 1 and Level 2 Advanced Training in Equine Facilitated Learning. I was about to embark on an eighteen month long EFL program as Program Co-ordinator. It suddenly dawned on me that really, while I might have helped saved Sophie's life in the physical sense, she had been instrumental in saving mine, in so many different ways. This work gave my life greater meaning and she was the key to it all. My life was full and rich in ways I had never dreamed possible when I decided to buy that orphaned filly so many years ago.

I knew that Sophie and I still had a long way to travel on our healing journey. However I could now see that we each had our own path to follow. Realizing this simple truth helped me to let go of any illusion of control in life. This included accepting that my brother was also on his own journey. I could not walk it for him, or fight his battles. The pain he, and those he cared about, experienced due to his mental health issues was no longer something to be afraid of. It was simply part of the journey. This gave me a sense of peace and comfort. I had learned how to set appropriate boundaries that enabled me to love and support him, without carrying a burden that was not mine to bear. I realized I had learned to trust. This trust helped me to forgive myself, and my former husband, for the heartache we had caused each other and to appreciate the experience of our marriage as being one thread in a rich, full and imperfect life.

What started out as a journey to help save a horse has led full circle back to horses helping heal humans, and it all started with one wild born, starving, orphaned horse who helped heal one broken hearted human.

Epilogue

Katherine's father had declined in health over the intervening years and she had made her peace with his passing long before he breathed his last. The finality of death is always unsettling. My whippet puppy, Monty the Brave, left this life long before I had even begun to make peace with his passing only a few days earlier, but that is another story.

Lilly gave birth to a beautiful Percheron filly in October 2012, having taken quite a shine to the beautiful Bardi when she met him in Dinninup – taking advantage of the opportunity her half sister Sophie had declined.

In August 2013 and in true Sophie style she delivered Aleppo in her time, and on her terms, with no-one around except the grey Earaheedy mares Margaret and Lorna. I felt this was how it should be. The young colt, although a little premature, is sassy and strong.

Photo Courtesy of Katherine Waddington
Sophie and Aleppo, August 2013

He named himself Aleppo before he was born. Aleppo's father is Cracker, the young colt rescued from Juna Downs and purchased by Katherine and Kevin. Sophie fell pregnant at the end of her second summer running with Cracker.

Interestingly, when Sophie returned from her sojourn to visit Bardi in 2011, an animal communicator (then a friend of a friend) advised me that Sophie had been confused about why she was sent to be with Bardi and that if Sophie was ever to fall pregnant she would do so after running for a year or two with a young colt-stallion.

Photo Courtesy of Katherine Waddington, Lilly and Skye, October 2012

The ongoing journey of self discovery and equine therapies continues to take me and my friends – horse and human – to amazing places. My herd of horses love their work as equine facilitators, as do many of Katherine and Kevin's horses. Their Wadi Farm property is now becoming a centre for individual, group and retreat programs for people wishing to experience insightful interactions with horses.

Photo Courtesy of Katherine Waddington, Elizabeth, Sophie, Carranya and the Earaheedy mares Margaret, Lorna and Darrah

About the Author

Elizabeth Denniss is a diploma qualified life coach, equine facilitator and project manager with 15 years experience in community development as well as personal coaching. She founded Rafa Life Inward Journey, a business aimed at promoting authentic living, after discovering the powerful way in which horses can help humans heal and grow. This awareness was developed through her own healing experiences with wild born horses.

Elizabeth is a former President of the Outback Heritage Horse Association of WA Inc, and an affiliate trainer with the Australian Equine Facilitated Learning Pty Ltd. Elizabeth lives in the picturesque south west corner of Western Australia with her herd of five horses and two dogs.